# Gifted and Talented Teens:
## Enhancing Strengths and Discovering Opportunities for Growth

REPRODUCIBLE SELF-ASSESSMENTS, EXERCISES & EDUCATIONAL HANDOUTS

## A Clinician's Guide

By Ester R.A. Leutenberg and
Carol Butler Cooper, MS Ed., RN, C

**Whole Person Associates**

101 West 2nd Street, Suite 203
Duluth, MN 55802-5004

800-247-6789

Books@WholePerson.com
WholePerson.com

**Gifted and Talented Teens: Enhancing Strengths and Discovering Opportunities for Growth Workbook**

Copyright ©2020 by Ester R.A. Leutenberg and
Carol Butler Cooper, MS Ed., RN, C
All rights reserved. The activities, assessment tools, and handouts in this book are reproducible by the purchaser for educational or therapeutic purposes. No other part of this book may be reproduced or transmitted in any form by any means, electronic, or mechanical without permission in writing from the publisher.

All efforts have been made to ensure the accuracy of the information contained in this book as of the date published. The authors and the publisher expressly disclaim responsibility for any adverse effects arising from the use or application of the information contained herein.

Editorial Director: Jack Kosmach
Art Director: Mathew Pawlak
Cover Design: Mathew Pawlak
Editor: Peg Johnson

Library of Congress Control Number: 2020932744
ISBN:978-1-57025-360-7

*From the co-authors, Ester and Carol*
*Our thanks to these professionals who share their expertise with us.*

Editor and Life-long Teacher – Eileen Regen, M Ed, CIE
Proof-reader and Reviewer – Jay Leutenberg, CASA
Reviewer, Teen Teacher, and Consultant – Niki Tilicki, MA Ed
Editorial Director – Jack Kosmach
Art Director – Mathew Pawlak
Copy Editor – Peg Johnson

*A Special Thank You
to
Whole Person Associates*

*for their interest in gifted and talented teens,
their families, and their facilitators.*

---

### Free PDF Download Available
To access your free PDF download of the assessment tools
and all of the reproducible activities in this workbook, go to:
**https://WholePerson.com/store/GiftedandTalentedTeens2744.html**

# Gifted and Talented Teens: Enhancing Strengths and Discovering Opportunities for Growth

## Introduction

**This book will help facilitators empower gifted and talented teens to enhance their strengths and discover opportunities for growth.**

Gifted and talented teens often have physical, emotional, and social challenges. They are exposed to an ever widening, diversified, and sometimes scary world. All adolescents may feel insecure, test boundaries, feel peer pressure, and wonder about their futures. Gifted and talented teens struggle with these same issues. They may excel in one or more area and struggle in others.

### Possible Characteristics Gifted and Talented Teens Possess and/or May Need to Work On

| | | |
|---|---|---|
| Ability to analyze | Emotional awareness | Perseverance |
| Acceptance | Empathy | Perspectives, broad or narrow |
| Achievement | Energy level changes | Preference to "coast" |
| Acting as class clown | Enthusiasm | Pressure |
| Advanced cognitive development | Expectations of others | Problem solving of strengths and weaknesses |
| Attention span | Expectations of self | |
| Attitude | Fears of failure | Questioning |
| Awareness of pressure to excel | Feelings of being different | Rejection |
| Boredom | Feelings of being misunderstood | Resistance toward team projects |
| Bossiness | Focus on issues | Self-reliance |
| Bullying | Friendships | Sense of humor |
| Burn-out | Frustration | Sensitivity to criticism |
| Challenging friendships | Independence | Sensitivity to surroundings |
| Competitiveness | Interests – varied or singular | Sensitivity to needs and needs of others |
| Concentration skills | Motivation | |
| Coping skills | Non-conformance | Social awareness |
| Creativity | Organizational skills | Solutions |
| Curiosity | Over-reactions | Special talents |
| Decision Making | Patience | Tolerance |
| Direction | Perfectionism | Varied or singular interests |
| Disruptive behaviors | | Worries about fitting in |

# Features of Gifted and Talented Teens: Enhancing Strengths and Discovering Opportunities for Growth

**A User-Friendly Resource**
Educators and counselors of gifted and talented teens, mental health professionals, and facilitators in virtually any setting will find this resource tailored to the strengths and needs of their clients.

**Adaptable**
The Facilitator's Possibilities page at the end of each activity suggests ways to present the Exercise(s) as well as follow-up possibilities. Each handout can stand alone or a chapter can become a series of sessions or a workshop.

**Age and Ability Appropriate**
Activities are for gifted and talented teens, and are adaptable to individual or group exercises, whether facilitator led or used as self-directed learning..

**Comprehensive Chapters**
Each chapter provides ten or more activities for each of the following topics:

1. **Intrapersonal and Interpersonal**
   Teens first focus on their qualities within, traits that benefit or deter their progress, the senselessness of comparisons, and character traits. Teens then explore their interactions with others, rapport, levels of conformity, friendships, and love relationships.
2. **Thought Power**
   Teens investigate their emotional intelligence, perspectives, and values, and they compare artificial to human intelligence. Teens identify and reprogram distorted thoughts and differentiate between distress and eustress.
3. **Giving Back**
   Teens re-gift an intangible quality, and explore ways to use their difficulties, talents, and resources to help others. Teens develop a personal platform, experience positive reciprocity, and find value in forgiveness.
4. **Team Player**
   Teens acknowledge that disagreements can lead to innovation, and conflicts can be resolved. Teens apply sportsmanship concepts to competitive situations and identify ways to manage wins, losses, and mistakes. Teens practice communication, leadership, and followership.
5. **Self-Expression**
   Teens share ideas about topics important to them through their choices of visual art, the written or spoken word, theater, dance, music, fantasy, and other techniques. Teens change self-limiting thoughts into personal power, identify insights, evoke emotions, and take healthy risks through creative expression.

**To encourage self-directed learning:**
- Distribute the Chapter Cover Pages, discuss the quotations and information, and let teens choose which chapter to experience next.
- Distribute the Table of Contents and let teens choose which activity to experience next.

*(Continued on the next page)*

# Features of Gifted and Talented Teens: Enhancing Strengths and Discovering Opportunities for Growth *(Continued)*

**Individualized**
A facilitator may adapt worksheets to best suit the participant(s).
Handouts can be individual worksheets to be shared with peers or professionals, or kept private.
Activities can be experienced individually.

**Motivating**
Facilitators may create their own approaches to meet their participants' needs.

**Interactive**
Activities can be experienced as a whole group process, teams, or pairs.

**Introspective**
All activities assist participants to gain insight and apply concepts to their lives.

**Reproducible**
The activity handouts are meant to be printed for distribution to participants.

**Time Saving Suggestion**
Facilitators can spend a few minutes preparing for a group or individual sessions by quickly reading the handout and reviewing the Facilitator's Possibilities found following each handout or set of handouts.

### The Modalities Used to Engage Teens with Varied Needs, Interests, and Preferences

- Abstraction
- Altruistic Expression
- Analogy
- Ask the Audience
- Brainstorming
- Case Studies
- Character Creation
- Cognitive Practice
- Collages
- Comic Strips
- Contests
- Continuums
- Creative Expression
- Cutouts
- Debates
- Discussions
- Fable Creation
- Fantasy
- Figures of Speech
- Flash Cards
- Followership
- Games
- Idiom Personalization
- Inner Dialog
- Journaling
- Leadership
- Limerick Composition
- Lyrics
- Pantomime
- Pass the Paper
- Peer-Led Question and Answer
- Personal Platforms
- Perspective
- Poetry Analysis
- Poetry Composition
- Presentations
- Quotation Analysis
- Quotation Composition
- Quotation Personalization
- Reality Shows
- Research
- Respectful Risk-Taking
- Role Empowerment
- Role Play
- Scenarios
- Self-Empowerment
- Self-Examination
- Simulations
- Skits
- Social Media
- Story-Telling
- Stream of Consciousness
- Thought Bubbles
- Vicarious Experiences
- Wall stations

*The Table of Contents on page ix lists the above modalities with their corresponding activities.*

# How to Use
# Gifted and Talented Teens: Enhancing Strengths and Discovering Opportunities for Growth

The **Table of Contents** provides the page title, page number, and modality.

Each **Chapter Cover Page** provides an information box about the topic's relevance and a quotation for discussion.

Each **Reproducible Activity** has one or more teen handout, to be printed for individuals, teams, games, and other activities, and adapted as needed by making changes and using the handout as the master for your group.

Each **Facilitator's Possibilities** page following each handout or set of handouts:

1. **Strengths and Opportunities:** *emphasize the important points.*
2. **Supplies:** *most require only the handout and pens or pencils, with some optional extras.*
3. **Inquisitive Minds:** *introductory, motivational question(s).*
4. **Suggestions:** *possible ways to present the material.*
5. **Independent and Team Projects:** *ways to adapt the activity for individuals or teams.*
6. **Individuals or Teams:** *follow-up activities or variations for individuals or teams.*

Use these activities as ...

**A beginning,** not the final word on a subject.
**A chance** for self-directed learning as teens choose topics and methods of expression.
**A stress reducer** for participants who write, draw, etc., without need for technical skills.
**A suggestion,** not a solution to complex issues.
**A teachable moment** when awareness clicks within the participants.
**A technique** to put participants front and center as they present their projects or perform.
**A therapeutic process** as the group members relate with understanding and empathy.
**A vehicle** to incorporate the facilitator's own style of education and counseling.
**An opportunity** to use professional judgment to adapt the material to meet participants' needs.
**An option** to save time and energy when preparing for and documenting interventions.

---

## Caution

If a teen discloses emotional issues or thoughts about harming self or others, refer the teen to the appropriate mental health professional. If anyone is in danger, call 911 or your local Emergency Services number. The teen may also be taken to the nearest hospital Emergency Department.

Ask participants to refrain from putting an arm around someone or handing a tissue box to a person who is upset or crying. These actions or comments, intended to comfort, can interrupt the flow of the moment.

Advise teens to use name codes in their written and spoken responses to ensure privacy for their friends, family, and others. Example: If Pat loves violin, use PLV.

# Ways to Promote Insight

**Spark Spontaneity**
Ask participants to share thoughts and feelings freely and without concern about grammar or artistic skills. Allow unedited text, improvisational role-plays, stick figure drawings, and poetry in any style.

**Elicit Rather than Tell**
People form their own conclusions when questions, discussion, debate, and other techniques foster insight.

**Allow Comfort Zones**
Some participants jump at leadership opportunities; others prefer to observe. Some like to share their work; others opt for privacy. Let participants be who they are at any given moment.

**Promote Moving Beyond a Comfort Zone**
When participants feel safe, suggest small steps outside their comfort zones. A former observer might decide to respond to a question, document a team's ideas, or lead a discussion.

**Peers Teach**
Without a formal teacher-student role, peers learn from each other through observation, listening, being heard, teamwork, caring, feeling cared about, trusting, and being trusted. They learn they are not alone in their experiences and emotions.

**Disclosure Precautions**
- Participants may or may not choose to share their thoughts, feelings, actions, writings, drawings, etc.
- Confidentiality must be emphasized. "What is said in this room stays in this room."
- Instruct participants to use name codes, not initials, when identifying someone on an activity handout.
- Risks to confidentiality include participants who do not understand its importance.
- Facilitator confidentially is important, unless there is a chance of harm to the participant or to others.
- A facilitator's appropriate self-disclosure may open the door to participants' appropriate self-disclosure.
- People who fear negative feedback or seek positive feedback may omit or embellish facts.
- Some issues are inappropriate for a group of people who have not had the same experience.
- Participants may be reluctant to write their activity handout responses if they think they must reveal their responses to others.

**Feedback Pros and Cons**
Feedback occurs when peers or facilitators comment about a participant's responses.
    **Pros**
        People listen more thoughtfully when feedback is expected.
        Feedback is often helpful if expressed kindly and carefully.
        Discussions about a person's responses elicit different ideas.
        Positive comments about a person's responses may lead to open-mindedness.
    **Cons**
        The value of sharing is the act of asserting personal ideas, not in receiving approval from listeners.
        There is freedom in knowing listeners will accept what is said without comment or advice.
        Negative, unkind feedback can be detrimental. Explanation of how to give feedback is essential.

**Catharsis: Let It Flow!**
Uninterrupted emotional release, amidst attentive listeners, promotes healing.

# Gifted and Talented Teens:
# Enhancing Strengths and Discovering Opportunities for Growth

# Table of Contents

## Introduction

Introduction – Gifted and Talented Teens: Enhancing Strengths and
Discovering Opportunities for Growth . . . . . . . . . . . . . . . . . . . . . . . . . . . . . . . . . . . . . . . . . . . iv

Features of Gifted and Talented Teens: Enhancing Strengths
and Discovering Opportunities for Growth . . . . . . . . . . . . . . . . . . . . . . . . . . . . . . . . . . . . . . v

How to Use Gifted and Talented Teens: Enhancing Strengths and
Discovering Opportunities for Growth. . . . . . . . . . . . . . . . . . . . . . . . . . . . . . . . . . . . . . . . . . vii

Ways to Promote Insight. . . . . . . . . . . . . . . . . . . . . . . . . . . . . . . . . . . . . . . . . . . . . . . . . . . . . . viii

Table of Contents . . . . . . . . . . . . . . . . . . . . . . . . . . . . . . . . . . . . . . . . . . . . . . . . . . . . . . . . . . . . . ix

# Gifted and Talented Teens:
## Enhancing Strengths and Discovering Opportunities for Growth

# Table of Contents

## Chapter 1 — INTRAPERSONAL AND INTERPERSONAL

**Modality**

| | | |
|---|---|---|
| Introduction | 15 | |
| Multifaceted Me – Features | 17 | Abstraction |
| Multifaceted Me – Factors | 18 | Analogy |
| Multifaceted Me – Pressure | 19 | Journaling |
| Facilitator Possibilities | 20 | |
| Perfectionism Presentations | 21 | Presentations |
| Facilitator Possibilities | 22 | |
| My Super Hero | 23 | Fantasy, Contest |
| Facilitator Possibilities | 24 | |
| Guess My Trait | 25 | Reality Show, Game |
| Facilitator Possibilities | 26 | |
| My Properties: Transparent, Translucent, Opaque | 27 | Abstraction |
| Ponder My Properties | 28 | Analogy |
| My Properties, Human Transparency, Translucency, and Opacity | 29 | Inner Dialog |
| Facilitator Possibilities | 30 | |
| People Will Never Forget | 31 | Quotation Personalization |
| Facilitator Possibilities | 32 | |
| RAP: Building Rapport | 33 | Role Play, Debate, Lyrics, Discussion |
| Facilitator Possibilities | 34 | |
| Fitting In: Fit In or Not? | 35 | Journaling |
| Fitting In: Helpful or Not Helpful? | 36 | Cutout Game |
| Fitting In: Isolated, Introverted, or Extraverted | 37 | Continuum |
| Facilitator Possibilities | 38 | |
| Fall into Friendship: Slowly Does It! | 39 | Quotation Personalization |
| Fall into Friendship: Maintain a Firm Friendship! | 40 | Self-Examination |
| Fall into Friendship: Constant or Not? | 41 | Quotation Composition |
| Facilitator Possibilities | 42 | |
| Love: Voice Your Views about Love | 43 | Poetry Analysis and Composition |
| Facilitator Possibilities | 44 | |

# Gifted and Talented Teens:
# Enhancing Strengths and Discovering Opportunities for Growth

# Table of Contents

## Chapter 2 — THOUGHT POWER

**Modality**

| | | |
|---|---|---|
| Introduction | 45 | |
| Emotional Intelligence | 47 | Self-Examination |
| Facilitator Possibilities | 48 | |
| What are You Thinking? Be a Thought-Bouncer | 49 | Thought Bubble |
| What are You Thinking? Recognize Thought Distortions | 50 | Cognitive Practice |
| What are You Thinking? Change Your Thoughts | 51 | Cognitive Practice |
| Facilitator Possibilities | 52 | |
| Recycle Your Troubles | 53 | Abstraction, Analogy |
| Facilitator Possibilities | 54 | |
| The Positive Realist | 55 | Character Creation, Role Play |
| Facilitator Possibilities | 56 | |
| Artificial Intelligence: Versus Human Intelligence | 57 | Self-Examination |
| Artificial Intelligence: Human Skills | 58 | Role Play, Brainstorm, Story-Telling |
| Artificial Intelligence: Values | 59 | Persuasion, Collage |
| Facilitator Possibilities | 60 | |
| Reprogram Your Irrational Thoughts | 61 | Cognitive Practice |
| Facilitator Possibilities | 62 | |
| What Do You Think About Stress? EUSTRESS | 63 | Self-Examination |
| What Do You Think About Stress? DISTRESS | 64 | Stream of Consciousness |
| What Do You Think About Stress? BUTTERFLIES | 65 | Limerick Composition |
| Facilitator Possibilities | 66 | |
| Shedding Light on the Subject | 67 | Idiom Personalization |
| Facilitator Possibilities | 68 | |
| Your Mind's Lens – Close-Up | 69 | Perspective: Close-Up |
| Your Mind's Lens – Panorama | 70 | Perspective: Big Picture |
| Your Mind's Lens – Magnify, Minimize, or Tunnel Vision? | 71 | Cognitive Practice |
| Facilitator Possibilities | 72 | |
| Your Values Indicator | 73 | Abstraction, Self-Examination |
| Facilitator Possibilities | 74 | |

# Gifted and Talented Teens:
# Enhancing Strengths and Discovering Opportunities for Growth

# Table of Contents

## Chapter 3 — GIVING BACK

**Modality**

| | | |
|---|---|---|
| Introduction | 75 | |
| Re-Gift | 77 | Creative Expression |
|    Facilitator Possibilities | 78 | |
| HELP is ON THE WAY! | 79 | Cutout Game |
|    Facilitator Possibilities | 80 | |
| Talents Used for a Cause - TALENTS | 81 | Self-Examination |
| Talents Used for a Cause - CAUSES | 82 | Altruistic Expression |
| Talents Used for a Cause - COMBINATIONS | 83 | Thought Cloud |
|    Facilitator Possibilities | 84 | |
| From Adversity to Advocacy | 85 | Case Study |
|    Facilitator Possibilities | 86 | |
| Philanthropy Fantasy | 87 | Simulation, Wall Stations |
|    Facilitator Possibilities | 88 | |
| Promote Your Platform | 89 | Personal Platform |
|    Facilitator Possibilities | 90 | |
| Gratitude Gives | 91 | Self-Examination |
|    Facilitator Possibilities | 92 | |
| Where Does Your Money Go? | 93 | Research, Presentation |
|    Facilitator Possibilities | 94 | |
| FORGIVENESS: The Gift that Gives Back | 95 | Peer Led Question and Answer |
|    Facilitator Possibilities | 96 | |
| Use Idioms to Give Back | 97 | Idiom Personalization |
|    Facilitator Possibilities | 98 | |

# Gifted and Talented Teens:
# Enhancing Strengths and Discovering Opportunities for Growth

# Table of Contents

## Chapter 4 — TEAM PLAYER

**Modality**

| | | |
|---|---|---|
| Introduction | 99 | |
| Agree to Disagree | 101 | Respectful Risk-Taking |
| Facilitator Possibilities | 102 | |
| Strategies for Conflict Resolution | 103 | Skits, Brainstorming |
| Facilitator Possibilities | 104 | |
| Time to Adapt? | 105 | Flash Cards, Pass the Paper |
| Facilitator Possibilities | 106 | |
| Sportsmanship Messages | 107 | Pantomime, Ask the Audience |
| Facilitator Possibilities | 108 | |
| Everyone Makes Mistakes | 109 | Fable Creation |
| Facilitator Possibilities | 110 | |
| Not Everyone Gets the Gold | 111 | Vicarious Experience |
| Facilitator Possibilities | 112 | |
| Followership Power | 113 | Role Empowerment |
| Facilitator Possibilities | 114 | |
| Challenge the Leader | 115 | Role Play: Leadership, Followership |
| Facilitator Possibilities | 116 | |
| Communication: Heart or Head First? | 117 | Scenario, Cutout Game |
| Facilitator Possibilities | 118 | |
| TOO Easily Offended? | 119 | Self-Examination, Comic Strip |
| Facilitator Possibilities | 120 | |

# Gifted and Talented Teens:
# Enhancing Strengths and Discovering Opportunities for Growth

# Table of Contents

## Chapter 5 — SELF-EXPRESSION

**Modality**

| | | |
|---|---|---|
| Introduction | 121 | |
| Your World | 123 | Quotation Personalization |
|    Facilitator Possibilities | 124 | |
| Individualized Initialisms | 125 | Initialism Personalization |
|    Facilitator Possibilities | 126 | |
| Teen Culture | 127 | Collage, Fantasy |
|    Facilitator Possibilities | 128 | |
| Speak Your Truth | 129 | Quotation Analysis and Composition |
|    Facilitator Possibilities | 130 | |
| Entelechy = You! | 131 | Abstraction, Self-Empowerment |
|    Facilitator Possibilities | 132 | |
| Limiting or Limitless? | 133 | Cognitive Practice |
|    Facilitator Possibilities | 134 | |
| Q&A: Site for Insight | 135 | Social Media, Peer Q & A |
|    Facilitator Possibilities | 136 | |
| EVOKE | 137 | Creative Expression |
|    Facilitator Possibilities | 138 | |
| Paraprosdokians | 139 | Figures of Speech Creation |
|    Facilitator Possibilities | 140 | |
| Creativity | 141 | Quotation Analysis, Self-Expression |
|    Facilitator Possibilities | 142 | |

CHAPTER 1

# Intrapersonal and Interpersonal

> *Intra*personal refers to thoughts, feelings, values, goals and other qualities within you. Understanding yourself helps you decide which intrapersonal traits to strengthen, diminish, or develop. The better you know yourself, the better you understand your reactions to, and your effects on, others. Insight enables you to direct your gifts and talents toward goals that you define for yourself.
>
> *Inter*personal refers to your interactions with others. Examining your connections with others helps you decide how to treat people, choose friends, and maintain quality relationships.

The more you know yourself,
the more patience you have for what you see in others.
**~ Erik Erikson**

In this chapter teens first focus on their qualities within, traits that benefit or deter their progress, the senselessness of comparisons, and character traits. They then explore their interactions with others, rapport, levels of conformity, friendships, and love relationships.

# Multi-Faceted Me — Features

You are a multi-faceted gem. Some facets are brilliant and some not as brilliant, and other facets may have little or big chips.

Below is another type of multi-faceted gem.
On each facet, describe one of your non-physical features.
Include some features that seem <u>brilliant</u> and some that have <u>chips</u>.
*Example of brilliant: Math is way too easy!*
*Example of chips: I feel awkward talking to someone I would like to get to know better.*

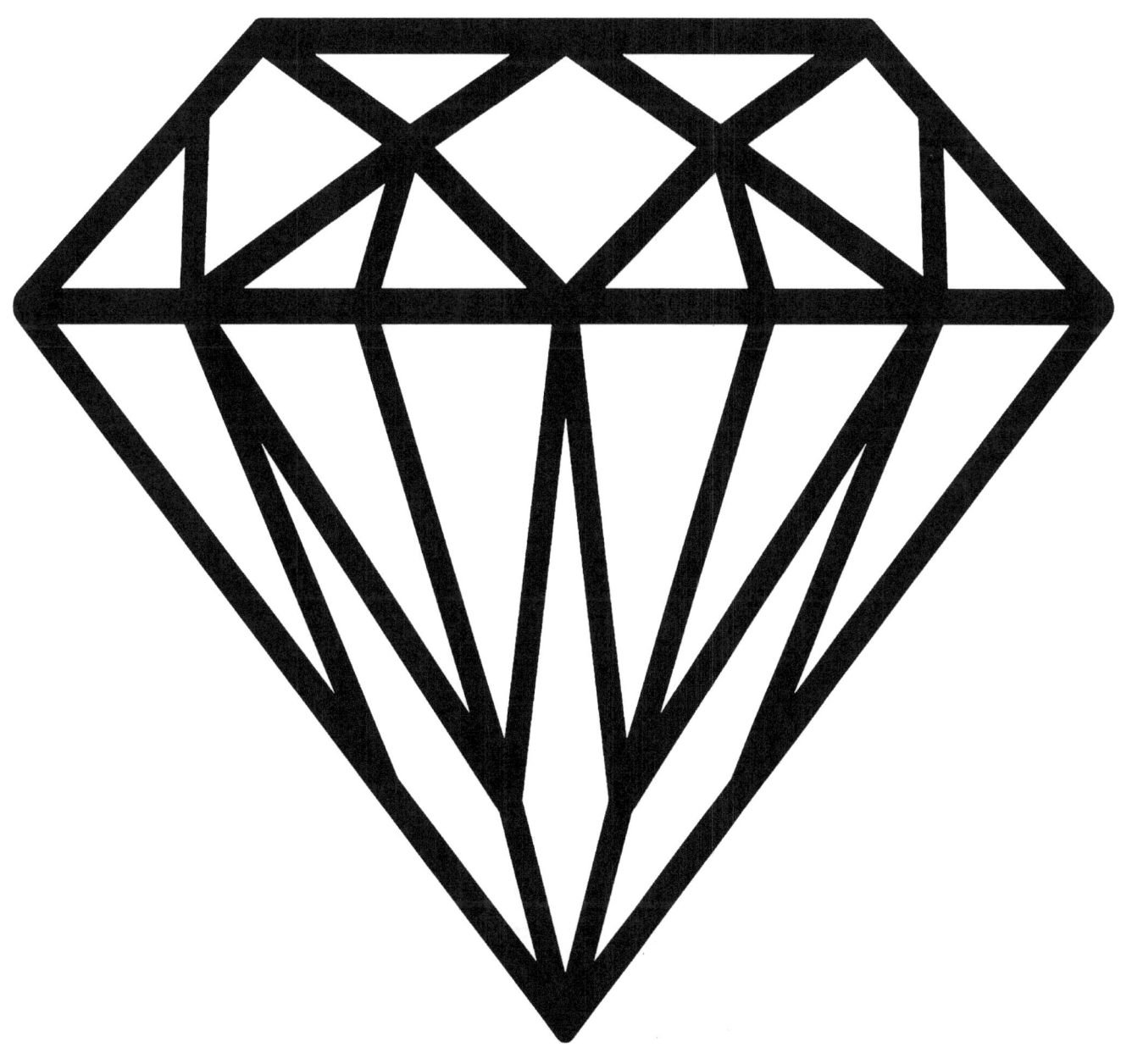

# Multi-Faceted Me – Factors

**You are a multi-faceted gem!**

Some facets form brilliant gems.
Describe factors that helped form your facets.

| Facet | Intrinsic Factors (built in or hard-wired) | Extrinsic Factors (originate from the outside) |
|---|---|---|
| Ex: Intelligence | I want to know "How?" and "Why?" | My teachers encourage me to find answers. |
| Ex: Impatience | I get really annoyed when people speak slowly. | My best friend pressures me to "Hurry up and get to the point!" |
| | | |
| | | |
| | | |
| | | |
| | | |
| | | |
| | | |

# Multi-Faceted Me – Pressure

### You are a multi-faceted gem!

Environmental pressure influences gem formation.
Your environment (peer pressure, family, media, etc.) may pressure you.

*My most positive non-physical feature is* _____.
*Environmental pressure influences this feature by …*

*My most troublesome non-physical feature is* _____.
*Environmental pressure influences this feature by …*

# Multi-Faceted Me - Facilitator Possibilities

**Strengths and Opportunities**
    Discover one's non-physical facets (traits) and identify formative factors.
    Identify ways a facet can be positive and negative depending on purpose and intensity.

**Supplies**
    Handouts and pens.

**Inquisitive Minds**
    Show a gemstone worn by the facilitator or a group member, or a picture of a gem.
    Ask, "How do gems form?" (temperature, pressure, chemistry, and other conditions)

**Suggestions**
    Prompt a discussion about physical traits and how they form through heredity and lifestyle.
    Distribute the three handouts and supplies.
    Remind participants to address positive and negative traits.
    After completion, volunteers share their work.

**Wrap-Up**
    Elicit that many features are both positive and negative depending on purpose and intensity.
    Encourage participants to brainstorm examples.
    Possibilities:
        Purpose – Intelligence can be used to save or destroy lives.
        Intensity – Generosity helps people in need but could foster dependency.

**Independent and Team Projects**
    **Independent**
        Participants complete the pages individually.

    **Team**
        Team members create and name a fictional character and complete the pages based on hypothetical features, factors, and conditions.

    **Individuals or Teams**
        Identify features they would like to acquire or augment.
        Research ways to develop these features.

# Perfectionism Presentations

**Thin Line Team**

There is a thin line between setting high standards for performance and expecting perfection.

**Effects Team**

Perfectionism can cause underachievement, physical, and emotional problems.

**Response Team**

You receive 93% on a test and someone says: "What about the other 7%?" Respond.

**Depersonalization Team**

It helps to recognize that a grade, appearance, size, a win, a loss, etc., does not define one's self-worth.

**Enough Is Enough**

It helps to know how much time and effort to put into each endeavor and when to move on..

**Progress Team**

Progress, not perfection, is the goal.

**Effects Team**

Perfectionism can cause underachievement, physical and emotional problems.

**Perseverance Team**

Thomas A. Edison said: *Success is one percent inspiration and ninety-nine percent perspiration.*

**Setback Team**

What appears to be a failure will be a valuable learning experience.

**Refinement Team**

Expect criticisms and suggestions. Revisions are part of the process in any endeavor.

**Bravery Team**

To try a task but not excel is brave, versus avoiding challenges due to fear of not being the best.

**Success Team**

Some people fear failure; others fear success because of future expectations.

**Other Team**

Present any other aspect of perfectionism not addressed on the above list..

# Perfectionism Presentations - Facilitator Possibilities

**Strengths and Opportunities**
    Recognize the positive and negative effects of perfectionism.

**Supplies**
    Handouts, pens, board, markers
    Optional: PowerPoint or other audio-visual materials.

**Inquisitive Minds**
    A volunteer asks, "What do you think about a person who strives to be a perfectionist?" Peers brainstorm while the volunteer lists their responses on the board.

**Suggestions**
    Distribute the handout.
    Emphasize that teams will plan interactive presentations with an audience of their peers.
    Encourage team formations with approximately the same numbers of participants in each.
    Team members collaborate, writing ideas on the backs of their handouts.
    Teams present their activities.

**Wrap-Up**
    Ask volunteers to share ideas and responses about the about their personal experiences with perfectionism.

**Independent and Team Projects**
    **Independent**
        Individuals instead of teams select and present or journal about a topic.

    **Team**
        The activity as suggested is a team project.

    **Individuals or Teams**
        Research famous people who took risks and faced failures that led to success.

# My Superhero

Create a Superhero between the ages of thirteen and eighteen to be
Entered in a city-wide Superhero contest!

Attribute one admirable trait to your Superhero
in each specific trait area.

Ability _____

Creativity _____

Character _____

Intellect _____

Talent _____

Personality _____

Add a trait _____


Give your Superhero a descriptive name:

_____

# My Superhero – Facilitator Possibilities

**Strengths and Opportunities**
    Acknowledge the futility of comparing apples and oranges *(different but equal traits)*.
    Identify detrimental effects of comparisons and ways to avoid them.

**Supplies**
    Opening page and Superhero handouts and pens.

**Inquisitive Minds**
    Ask, "Who was the first Superhero you knew as a child?"
        "What traits did this Superhero possess?"

**Suggestions**
    Distribute the opening page and Superhero handouts.
    After everyone has completed the handouts, a volunteer from each side of the room will collect their Superhero handouts.
    The two volunteers exchange piles of handouts and return to their seats.
    Each side of the room forms a team.
    Each team evaluates the completed handouts they received from the other side.
    Each team discusses their own Superhero and his or her traits.
    Each team chooses a winner from the combined list of Superheroes.
    The group reconvenes and does not reveal their teams' winners.
        1. What difficulties did you encounter when trying to name the winner?
        2. What was easy for your team to agree on?
        3. What did you learn from this activity?
    Elicit that the uniqueness of individuals makes comparisons impossible.

**Wrap-Up**
    Just for fun ... if the teams arrived at a conclusion about which Superhero was best, identify the winner to the other team.

**Independent and Team Projects**
    **Independent**
        Participants journal about their own experiences when they have compared themselves with others.

    **Team**
        Team members discuss the detrimental effects of comparisons,
            *Ex: focus on what cannot be controlled, resentment, dissatisfaction, etc.*

    **Individuals or Teams**
        Research ways to avoid comparisons and appreciate personal attributes.

# Guess My Trait

| Industrious | Ethical | Creative |
|---|---|---|
| Inclusive | Collaborative | Humble |
| Generous | Optimistic | Determined |
| Brave | Open-minded | Empathic |

# Guess My Trait - Facilitator Possibilities

### Strengths and Opportunities
    Identify positive character traits
    Acknowledge one's own character traits.

### Supplies
    Scissors for the facilitator to cut out the boxes on the handout.
    Guess my Trait handout and pens for independent projects.

### Inquisitive Minds
    Ask, "How do you find out who a person really is?"

### Suggestions
    Before the session photocopy enough handouts for each participant to have one box.
        *Ex: one page for twelve participants, two pages for thirteen to twenty-four, etc.*
    Cut out the boxes; place cutouts face-down in a pile.
    Explain that a stack of character traits will be passed around.
    Participants each take one and do not reveal the trait to peers.
    Explain: "You are going to pretend to be on a reality show and have been told to plan an event that will reveal your character trait."
    A volunteer asks peers for event ideas *(Ex: party, class trip, service project)* and chooses one.
    If possible, participants place their chairs in a circle conducive to conversation.
    A volunteer calls on people who share ideas that demonstrate their trait without naming it.
        *Ex: the brave person suggests a healthy risk, the generous person praises a peer's idea.*
    After participants have each spoken once or twice, they guess each other's traits.

### Wrap-Up
    Play: *Guess the Trait*
    Participants decide on a secret positive trait (already addressed or any other positive trait).
    Participants share a short scenario about a person who displays the secret trait.
    Peers guess the trait that was described.

### Independent and Team Projects
**Independent**
    Participants receive an uncut handout and write in each box the ways they do and/or do not demonstrate the trait.

**Team**
    Team members discuss negative character traits and ways to diminish them

**Individuals or Teams**
    Research the character traits of leaders, visionaries, inventors, etc.

# My Properties: Transparent, Translucent, Opaque

Your properties, just like the properties of matter,
may be transparent, translucent or opaque.
They may be perceived as positive, negative, or both,
depending on their intensity and situation.

On the outside layer, note your non-physical qualities that are easily seen - transparent.
On the middle layer note your qualities that are not clearly visible unless one looks closely - translucent.
On the inner layer, note your qualities that are hidden from yourself or others, or private - opaque.

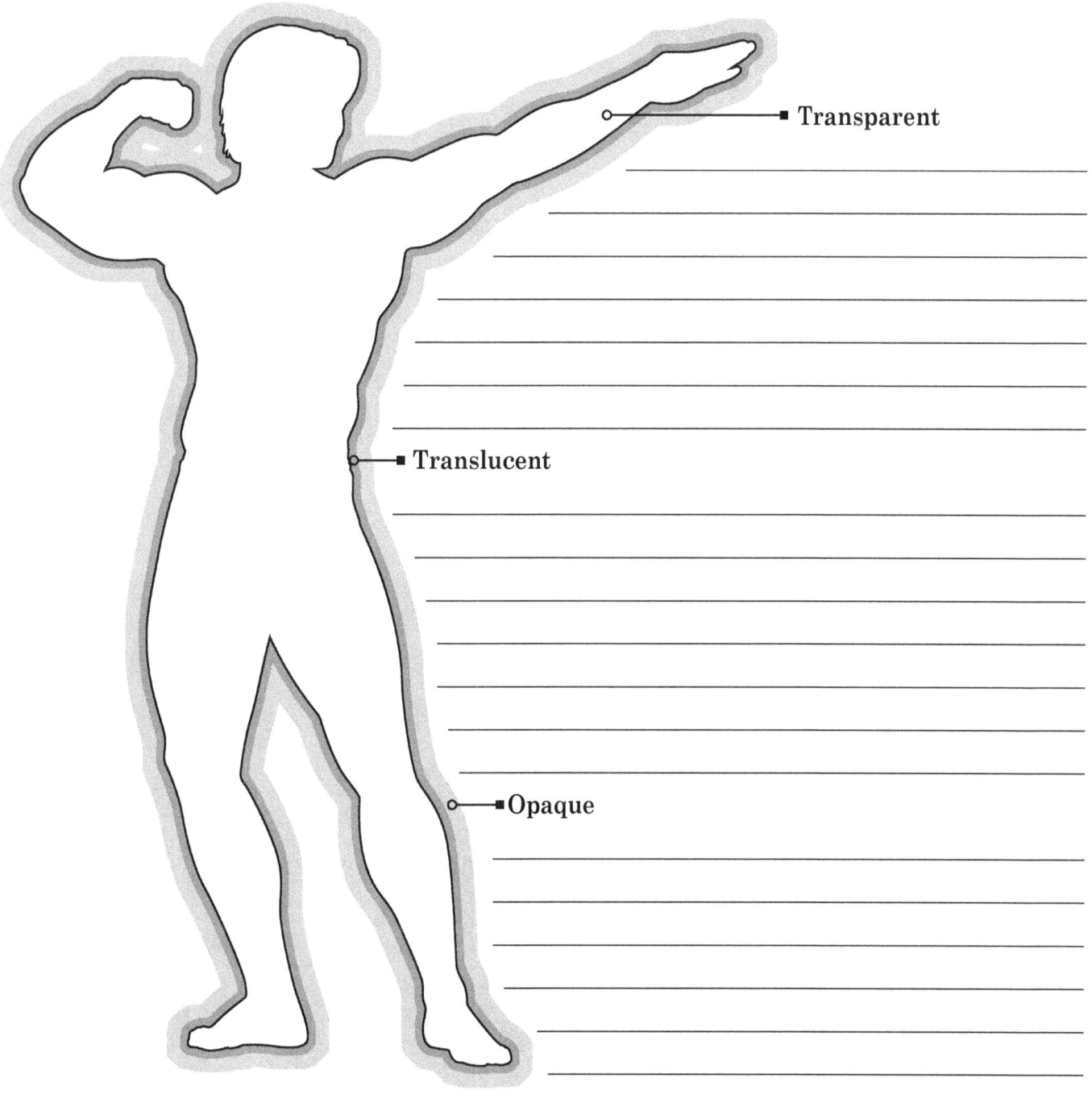

# Ponder My Properties

**Transparent (easy to perceive or detect)**
**Translucent (semi-transparent)**
**Opaque (not easy to see through)**

Which of your qualities would you like to be more transparent to yourself and why?

Which of your qualities would you like to be more transparent to others and why?

Which of your qualities would you like to be less transparent to yourself and why?

Which of your qualities would you like to be less transparent to others and why?

Which opaque qualities have you hidden from yourself and why?

Which opaque qualities have you hidden from others and why?

Give an example of transparency in one of your relationships *(family, friends, etc.)*.

Give an example of translucency in one of your relationships *(family, friends, etc.)*.

Give an example of opacity in one of your relationships *(family, friends, etc.)*.

In what ways can you, when appropriate, be transparent and yet maintain your privacy?

In what ways can you, when appropriate, be translucent and yet maintain your privacy?

In what ways can you, when appropriate, can you be opaque and yet have a meaningful relationship?

# My Properties: Human Transparency, Translucency, and Opacity

Express your inner dialogue by writing freely: unstructured, unedited, in any shape.
No rules! Write as your thoughts flow.
Start with the topic of *Human Transparency, Translucency and Opacity*

| **Transparent** *(easy to perceive or detect)* • **Translucent** *(semi-transparent)* • **Opaque** *(not easy to see through)* |
|---|

You *may* stray from the topic to wherever your thoughts may lead you.

# My Properties - Facilitator Possibilities

**Strengths and Opportunities**
>Identify personal *transparent, translucent,* and *opaque* qualities and their implications.

**Supplies**
>My Properties handouts, pens.
>Optional: Art supplies.

**Inquisitive Minds**
>Ask, "What are the properties of matter?"
>Volunteers define *transparent, translucent* and *opaque.*
>Ask, "In what ways could these terms apply to humans?"
>>Elicit: People's positive traits may be purposely transparent while they try to hide negative traits.
>
>Transparent qualities are not always positive and opaque qualities are not necessarily negative.
>>*Ex: A person could portray a tough facade, yet be tender-hearted.*

**Suggestions**
>Distribute the three handouts.
>Tell participants their work is private unless they decide to share with a trusted person.

**Wrap-Up**
>Ask for a show of hands of participants who strayed from the topic on the free-writing page.
>Volunteers share ideas, insights, or discoveries about their thoughts.

**Independent and Team Projects**
**Independent**
>Each page as presented can be an independent project.
>On the back of the pages, participants journal about ways they can transparently exemplify one of their positive opaque traits and eliminate a negative trait.

**Team**
>Team members create a fictitious person whose transparent traits are seemingly negative and opaque qualities are positive, then share their creations.

**Individuals or Teams**
>Create a person as described in the team section above.
>Create a short story, play, or cartoon showing how the person brought to the surface the hidden positive traits, or how someone else discovered the person's inner positive traits.

# People Will Never Forget

People will forget what you said, people will forget what you did,
But people will never forget how you made them feel.
~ **Maya Angelou**

| How do you think most people feel about themselves when they are in your presence? | Explain | What does it say about you if people feel good about themselves when they are with you? | Explain |
|---|---|---|---|
|  |  |  |  |

# People Will Never Forget - Facilitator Possibilities

**Strengths and Opportunities**
    Identify one's effect on others' self-concepts.
    Identify ways to contribute to others' positive feelings.

**Supplies**
    People Will Never Forget handout and pens.
    Board and marker.

**Inquisitive Minds**
    Write on the board: Who is responsible for your feelings?
    Elicit: People are responsible for their own feelings.
    No one can *make* a person feel a certain way without the person's permission.
    Yet, … people *can* influence others' feelings.

**Suggestions**
    Distribute the handout.
    After completion, volunteers share their responses.
    A volunteer asks the following question and lists peers' ideas on the board. "What are social cues"
    Participants may note facial expression, body language, tone of voice, posture, proximity, etc.

**Wrap-Up**
    Volunteers share stories about times they felt uncomfortable in someone's presence.
    Volunteers share stories about times they felt amazing in someone's presence.

**Independent and Team Projects**
    **Independent**
        Participants journal about people whom they have helped to feel more positive.

    **Team**
        Teams perform skits showing how to contribute to others' positive feelings.

    **Individuals or Teams**
        Research the cultural aspects of social cues, e.g., personal space, eye contact, etc.

# RAP - Building Rapport

**RAP =** Prior to becoming synonymous with rap music, rap was, and still is, known as talking in an easy and familiar manner.

**RAPPORT =** a close and harmonious relationship in which people understand each other's feelings and/or ideas, and communicate well.

## Choose Your Rap:

1. **Rap Session** *(Informal or unstructured group discussion.)*
   Join or start a rap session about ways to build rapport with people who seem different from you.
   Ideas:_____
   _____
   _____

2. **Interest Rap** *(Show interest in another person's thoughts, feelings, and activities.)*
   Rap with a peer to show interest.
   Ideas:_____
   _____
   _____

3. **Empathy Rap** *(Show that you understand another person's feelings.)*
   Rap with a person who is facing a challenge.
   Ideas:_____
   _____
   _____

4. **Bad Rap** *(Choose a position to substantiate and debate the opposition.)*
   Yes or No: Teens get a bad rap regarding their social skills.
   Ideas:_____
   _____
   _____

5. **Rap = Rhythm And Poetry** *(Compose.)*
   Create rap lyrics addressing ways to develop rapport.
   Ideas:_____
   _____
   _____

6. **Does rap music get a bad rap?** *(Explore.)*
   Open-mindedly explore the sophisticated rhyme forms, metaphors, and similes of rap music, as well as some of its criticisms.
   Ideas:_____
   _____
   _____

# RAP - Building Rapport - Facilitator Possibilities

**Strengths and Opportunities**
   Identify ways to build rapport with others.

**Supplies**
   Rap: Building Rapport handout and pens.

**Inquisitive Minds**
   Ask, "What is rapport?" and "When do you need to develop rapport with people?"

**Suggestions**
   Distribute the Rap: Building Rapport handout.
   Participants who choose numbers 1–4 form teams or work with partners.
   Participants who choose numbers 5–6 may work individually or with others.
   Team members and partners meet briefly to plan their rap demonstrations.
   Individuals complete their writing on the backs of the handouts.
   Participants perform their role-plays, debates, and share their lyrics and research.
   Peer audiences may provide feedback.

**Wrap-Up**
   Encourage a discussion by prompting teens to explain their opinions regarding this question, "Do you think teens with extraordinary talents find it easier or more difficult to put themselves in someone else's shoes?"

**Independent and Team Projects**
   **Independent**
      Participants sketch a scenario showing them developing rapport in a challenging situation
   **Team**
      Teams discuss idioms about rapport, *Ex: on the same wave length*.
      Team members share personal examples of the idiom in action.

   **Individuals or Teams**
      Journal privately or share with peers a story about a time they felt accepted, understood, and respected by someone they had known briefly.
      Journal or discuss ways to have empathy for someone's difficulty without becoming too emotionally involved.

# Fitting In: Fit In or Not to Fit In?

We all have times when we have negative or uneasy feelings and/or react negatively, uneasily, or cautiously because we just don't fit in!

*Describe how you felt and how you reacted in each of your fitting-in situations below.*

| A time I conformed in order to fit in | A time I ignored who I really am in order to fit in | A time I had hurt feelings because I did not fit in | A time I was sad because I did not fit in | A time I was glad because I did not fit in |
|---|---|---|---|---|
| | | | | |

## Gifted and Talented Teens Workbook — INTRAPERSONAL AND INTERPERSONAL

# Fitting In: Helpful or Not Helpful?

Fitting In: Helpful or Not Helpful?
In each section below, write a one-sentence scenario
that illustrates whether fitting in was helpful, or was not helpful.
Cut on the dashed lines and place the cutouts in a stack.
Players will pick up a cutout, read aloud, and ask: "Helpful or Not Helpful?"

*Ex: Pat goes to extremes to show individuality in every situation.* **(Not Helpful.)**
*Ex: Blair avoids people because of feeling "different."* **(Not Helpful.)**
*Ex: Addison prefers rock but goes with friends to a country music concert.* **(Helpful)**

✂----------------------------------------------------------------

**Scenario**

✂----------------------------------------------------------------

**Scenario**

✂----------------------------------------------------------------

**Scenario**

✂----------------------------------------------------------------

**Scenario**

✂----------------------------------------------------------------

**Scenario**

✂----------------------------------------------------------------

**Scenario**

✂----------------------------------------------------------------

**Scenario**

# Fitting In: Isolated, Introverted, or Extraverted?

- **Isolated** – Feels cut-off, lonely, and possibly rejected.
- **Introvert** – Prefers and is energized by time alone to pursue interests; reflective and reserved.
- **Extravert** – Prefers and is energized by large social gatherings; gregarious and unreserved.

*Place an x on the continuum in the location that best describes you.*

| ISOLATED | INTROVERTED | EXTRAVERTED |

Elaborate about your levels of feeling isolated, introverted, and extraverted.

☺ ME

# Fitting In: - Facilitator Possibilities

## Strengths and Opportunities
Identify how fitting in or not fitting in can lead to positive and/or negative emotions.

## Supplies
Fitting In handouts and pens.
Scissors to cut the *Fitting In: Helpful of Not Helpful?* slips of paper.

## Inquisitive Minds
Ask, "What issues do you think teens face when trying to fit in?"
Elicit that it depends on where and with whom they try to fit in, etc.

## Suggestions
Distribute the Fitting In handouts listed below:
*Fitting In: Fit In or Not?* Participants complete the page; volunteers share their responses.
*Fitting In: Helpful or Not Helpful?*
Refer to examples and ask participants' opinions.
Elicit that in the example of Pat, due to contrived uniqueness, Fitting In is probably not helpful.
- Participants write scenarios; scenarios are cut, collected, shuffled, and placed in a stack.
- Volunteers pick up a cutout, read aloud, and state whether the scenario is helpful or not helpful.
- Expect and allow discussion and debate as many interpretations as possible.

*Fitting In: Isolated, Introverted, or Extraverted*: Participants complete the page; volunteers share their responses.

## Wrap-Up
Draw a continuum on the board. Ask participants to form a horizontal line at the front of the room by placing themselves at their continuum locations.
Discuss the findings (many may be clustered at one end, some may fall in the middle, etc.).

## Independent and Team Projects
### Independent
Journal about sadness that stems from blaming self (for feeling different, etc.) or aggression that stems from blaming others (for rejection, etc.) and ways to overcome these (counseling, self-acceptance, tolerance for others who don't understand, etc.)

### Team
Panels discuss the issues addressed above under Independent.

### Individuals or Teams
Individuals write or teams share their opinions about extreme non-conformity:
*Cultivated Weirdness:* Examples, Pros, Cons, etc.

# Fall into Friendship: Proceed Slowly and Carefully

Be slow to fall into friendship; but when thou art in,
continue firm and constant.
### ~Socrates

*You may have fallen into a friendship that turned out well,
or into a friendship that did not!*

Reading Socrates quotation in the box above, what does it mean to fall into friendship? _____

_____
_____
_____
_____
_____

Give an example of falling into a friendship in your life. _____

_____
_____
_____
_____
_____

Why is it a good idea to go slowly with a new friend? _____

_____
_____
_____
_____
_____

What would be important for you personally to know about a friend before you become close and confide personal information? _____

_____
_____
_____
_____
_____

# Fall into Friendship: Maintain a Firm Friendship!

Be slow to fall into friendship; but when thou art in,
continue firm and constant.
~**Socrates**

The traits below help continue and maintain a firm friendship.
Near each trait below, note an example of a way you can exemplify that trait,
or of a way you do not exemplify that trait.

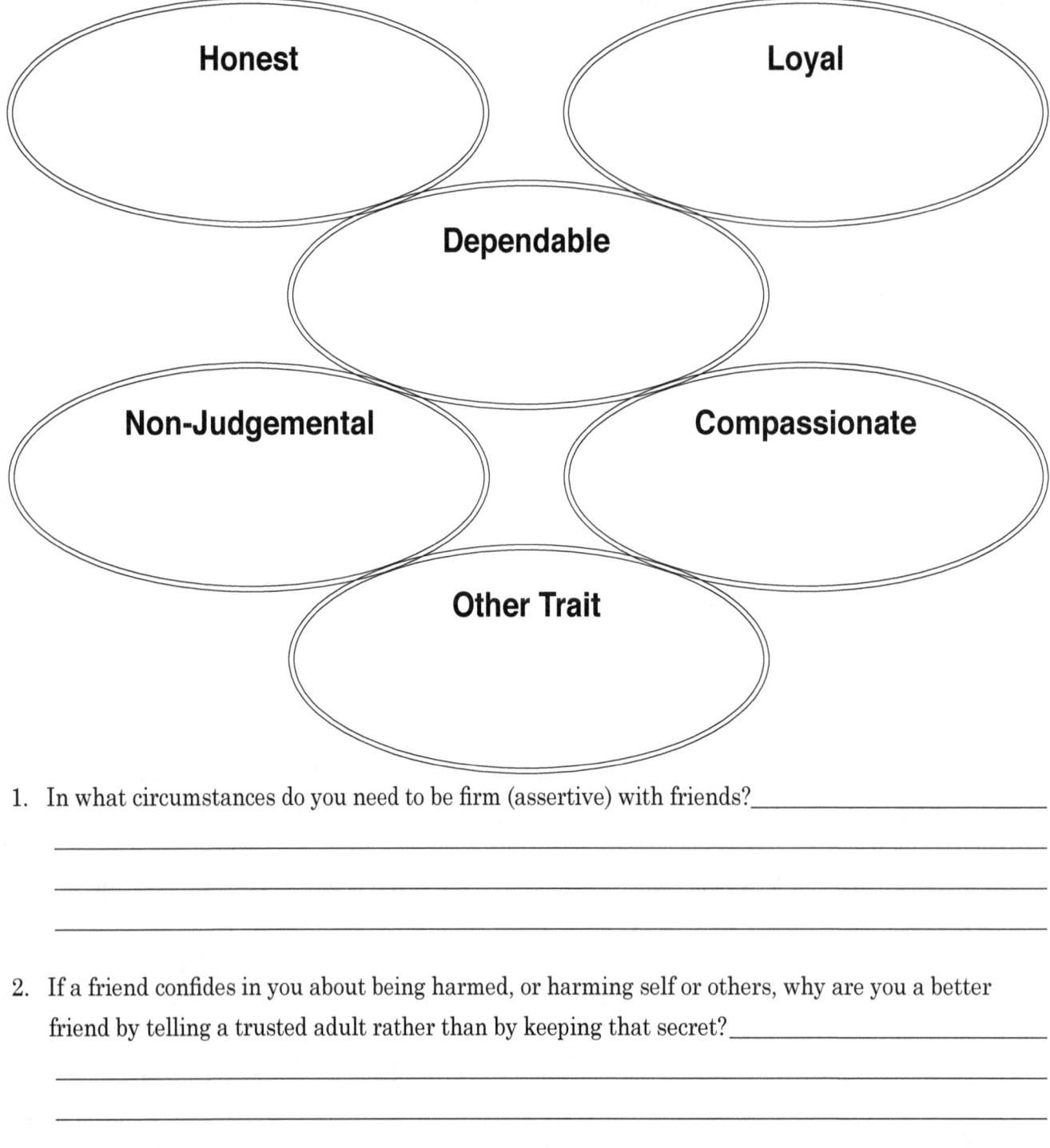

1. In what circumstances do you need to be firm (assertive) with friends? _____
   _____
   _____
   _____

2. If a friend confides in you about being harmed, or harming self or others, why are you a better friend by telling a trusted adult rather than by keeping that secret? _____
   _____
   _____
   _____

# Fall into Friendship: Constant or Not?

*Be slow to fall into friendship; but when thou art in,
continue firm and constant.*
**~Socrates**

1. What does the above quotation mean to you? _____
   _____
   _____

2. Do you agree with Socrates? _____   Explain: _____
   _____
   _____
   _____

3. Some signs that a friendship is worth keeping : friends positively influence each other, both make an effort to keep in touch, they are honest, supportive, and keep drama to a minimum. Describe a friendship you have that is worth keeping.
   _____
   _____
   _____

4. Name two circumstances in which you would NOT continue a friendship, even if the person were your best friend, and describe why not.

   1. _____
   _____

   2. _____
   _____

Compose your own words of wisdom about friendship.

# Fall into Friendship? - Facilitator Possibilities

### Strengths and Opportunities
Identify reasons and ways to choose friends wisely.

### Supplies
Handouts and pens.
White board or poster board and markers.

### Inquisitive Minds
Ask volunteers to share stories about friendships that seemed to start by chance.
Ask volunteers to share stories of times they *fell into a friendship or relationship* too easily.

### Suggestions
Distribute the three Friendship handouts.
After completion, volunteers share their responses to any items except their words of wisdom.
Emphasize the qualities of friendship.
Discuss the reasons to end a friendship, even if the person is a close or best friend.

### Wrap-Up
Volunteers print their words of wisdom on the white or poster board.
Participants discuss ways to apply the wisdom to their lives.
Participants may photograph the white board, then print or save in their phones.
The poster board may be the beginning of a bulletin board about friendship.

### Independent and Team Projects
#### Independent
Each page as presented is an individual project.
#### Team
Participants form three teams.
Each team receives one of the handouts.
Team members collaborate to complete their handout.
The group reconvenes; teams present their responses and may receive peer feedback.

#### Individuals or Teams
Individuals or teams create cartoons or story boards about friendships.
*Possibilities:* Friendships that start in unusual ways, last a lifetime, end early, etc.

# Voice Your Views about Love

### The Clod and the Pebble
By William Blake

Love seeketh not itself to please,
Nor for itself hath any care,
But for another gives its ease,
And builds a heaven in hell's despair.

So sang the little clod of clay,
Trodden with the cattle's feet;
But a pebble of the brook
Warbled out these metres meet:

Love seeketh only self to please,
To bind another to its delight,
Joys in another's loss of ease,
And builds a hell in heaven's despite.

*Now, write your own poem, and voice your view about love.*

_____
_____
_____
_____
_____
_____
_____
_____
_____
_____
_____
_____
_____
_____

# Voice Your Views about Love - Facilitator Possibilities

**Strengths and Opportunities**
Recognize aspects of selfless versus selfish love.

**Supplies**
Handouts and pens.

**Inquisitive Minds**
Ask, "What is the difference between a clod of clay and a pebble?"
*The clay is soft and malleable, the pebble is hard, worn down by erosion.*

**Suggestions**
Distribute the handout.
After a volunteer reads the poem aloud, ask participants to compare the clod and the pebble:
*The clod sees love as selfless, the pebble sees love as selfish.*
Ask, "What could have happened to each to form their views?"
*The clod may be idealistic, optimistic, never was hurt, or accepts being stepped on.*
*The pebble may be cynical, may have been mistreated by a selfish or cruel partner.*
Participants may use William Blake's format, or any rhyme scheme to compose their own poem.
Volunteers share their compositions.

**Wrap-Up**
Ask participants to give examples for the following:
*Healthy* selfishness in a romantic relationship
*Appropriate* selflessness in a romantic relationship.

**Independent and Team Projects**
**Independent**
Individuals journal ways they act selflessly or selfishly in relationships.
Individuals describe ways people they love(d) act selflessly or selfishly.
**Team**
Teams perform skits showing examples of different types of partners.
Those who are taken advantage of because of being too selfless.
Those who are unable to maintain a relationship due to excessive selfishness.

**Individuals or Teams**
Create a third character who is neither clod nor pebble but who exemplifies appropriate selflessness and healthy selfishness.

CHAPTER 2

# Thought Power

You cannot always control circumstances, but you can control and reframe your thoughts. Your thoughts influence your feelings, decisions, actions, and may affect the outcomes.

As a gifted and talented teen, you are well-equipped to reprogram self-defeating thoughts, differentiate between *dis*tress (anxiety-producing stress) and *eus*tress (exciting, positive stress), view your life from different perspectives, choose, and live up to your values.

I always like to look on the optimistic side of life, but I am realistic enough to know that life is a complex matter.
~ **Walt Disney**

In this chapter teens investigate their emotional intelligence, perspectives, and values, and they compare artificial to human intelligence. Teens identify and reprogram distorted thoughts and differentiate between distress and eustress.

# Emotional Intelligence

Emotional intelligence may contribute more to
your success than intellect (IQ).

*In order to recognize your own emotional intelligence,
complete the sentences below about incidents that happened to you.*

### 1. Self-Awareness

A time that I recognized an emotion as soon as it occurred: _____
_____

### 2. Self-Regulation

A time that I managed my impulses: _____
_____

A time that I adapted to change: _____
_____

A time that I was open to new ideas: _____
_____

### 3. Motivation

A time that I motivated myself to take appropriate action: _____
_____

### 4. Empathy

A time that I imagined how someone else felt: _____
_____

A time that I was able to help a person in distress without becoming overly stressed myself: _____
_____
_____

### 5. Social Skills

A time that I was able to negotiate a conflict: _____
_____

# Emotional Intelligence – Facilitator Possibilities

**Strengths and Opportunities**
Recognize self-awareness, self-regulation, motivation, empathy, and social skills.

**Supplies**
Emotional Intelligence handouts, pens.

**Inquisitive Minds**
Ask, "What is EQ?" *(The ability to recognize one's own and others' emotions and use the info to guide thoughts and behavior.)*

**Suggestions**
Distribute the Emotional Intelligence handout.
Volunteers share their responses.

**Wrap-Up**
Ask, "What is the downside of empathy?"
*(Feeling another's distress so deeply that the empathic person feels equally distressed.)*
Ask, "How can you show empathy without being negatively affected?"
*(Recognize that you care but are personally okay; take positive action to help, etc.)*

**Independent and Team Projects**

**Independent**
The page as presented is an independent project.
On the back of the page, participants journal about times they did not demonstrate emotional intelligence and what they could have done better in that situation.

**Team**
Teams research and present different aspects of emotional intelligence through infomercials or skits.

**Individuals or Teams**
Create a story about a character who does not demonstrate emotional intelligence.
Create a story about a character who demonstrates emotional intelligence.

# What Are You Thinking? Be a Thought-Bouncer

**Bouncers at concerts are on guard
to keep troublemakers out or remove them from the premises.**

**You can be a thought-bouncer by being on guard
and aware of thoughts that will cause trouble if you let them into your head.**

*Write a troublesome thought in the bubble.*

*What feelings result from this thought?*

_____
_____
_____
_____

*What actions or non-action can occur if you dwell on this thought?*

_____
_____
_____
_____

# What Are You Thinking? Recognize Thought Distortions

*Give an example of each type of negative thought distortion:*

**Filtering** – ignoring the positives and focusing on the negatives of a situation.
*Example:* _____
_____

**Polarization** – thinking in extremes of terrific or terrible, ignoring the middle ground.
*Example:* _____
_____

**Overgeneralization** – believing something that happened once will always reoccur.
*Example:* _____
_____

**Mind Reading** – assuming what others are thinking (often negative thoughts about oneself).
*Example:* _____
_____

**Catastrophizing** – fearing the worst possible outcome, "What if …"
*Example:* _____
_____

**Blaming** – pointing a finger at yourself or others for unfavorable outcomes.
*Example:* _____
_____

**Should** – believing a list of ironclad rules about how other people "should" act.
*Example:* _____
_____

**External Change** – thinking if others or situations change, that all will be well within yourself.
*Example:* _____
_____

**Labeling** – calling yourself, others, or circumstances, negative names.
*Example:* _____
_____

**Always Right** – needing to win every disagreement regardless of its importance.
*Example:* _____
_____

**Rewards** – expecting external rewards or recognition for every job well done.
*Example:* _____
_____

# What Are You Thinking? Change Your Thoughts

*In the box below, write a thought that does, or could, distress you.*

```
┌─────────────────────────────────────────────────────────────────────┐
│                                                                     │
│                                                                     │
│                                                                     │
│                                                                     │
└─────────────────────────────────────────────────────────────────────┘
```

*Practice these steps to change your thinking.*

In what way(s) is the thought in the box distorted? _____
_____
_____

What evidence supports this thought? _____
_____
_____

What evidence causes you to question this thought? _____
_____
_____

What harm do you do to yourself by thinking this way? _____
_____
_____

What would you tell a best friend who had this thought? _____
_____
_____

Write an argument to refute this thought. _____
_____
_____

Write a more positive but realistic thought replacement. _____
_____
_____

What do you gain by thinking this way? _____
_____
_____

# What Are You Thinking? – Facilitator Possibilities

**Strengths and Opportunities**
Recognize and refute one's troublesome thoughts.

**Supplies**
Three What Are You Thinking handouts and pens, board, and marker.
Slips of paper for the wrap-up.

**Inquisitive Minds**
Copy onto the board:
*There is nothing either good or bad but thinking makes it so.* ~ William Shakespeare.
Ask participants to explain whether they agree or disagree, and why.

**Suggestions**
Distribute the three What Are You Thinking handouts to participants.
After completion, volunteers share their responses.

**Wrap-Up**
Participants write distorted negative thoughts on slips of paper and place them in a stack.
Volunteers read the thoughts aloud and compose positive, realistic replacements.

**Independent and Team Projects**

**Independent**
The pages as presented are independent projects.
Individuals can journal about a current difficulty, the accompanying thoughts and feelings, and ways to change these responses.

**Team**
Team members complete the pages collaboratively.

**Individuals or Teams**
Research the work of Aaron Beck, MD, Albert Ellis, PhD, and David Burns, MD, who were instrumental in identifying the impact of thoughts on feelings and actions.

# Recycle Your Troubles

Troubles are like trash...we want to get rid of them quickly and forget about them...or do we?
Ecology says to recycle our trash into something useful.
Wisdom says to recycle our troubles, to learn from them and improve.

Label the trash can with a recent or current trouble over which you have significant control.

*Example for trash can – My last friendship ended because I argued over every little thing.*

*Example for recycling the experience – I ignore small annoyances and calmly discuss bigger issues in my current friendships.*

*In what ways can you recycle your experience in order to keep yourself out of trouble?*

_____
_____
_____

# Recycle Your Troubles - Facilitator Possibilities

## Strengths and Opportunities
Recognize lessons learned from troublesome experiences.
Recognize the benefits of sharing difficulties with others.

## Supplies
Recycle Your Troubles handout and pens.
Board and marker.

## Inquisitive Minds
Ask, "How can positive experiences be recycled?"
> *(photos, social media posts, journal entries, etc.).*

Ask, "How can troublesome experiences be recycled?"
> *(learn from mistakes, gain strength from adversity).*

## Suggestions
Distribute the Recycle your Troubles handout.
After completion, volunteers share their responses.

## Wrap-Up
Ask a volunteer to write on the board, "Don't sweep it under the rug."
Elicit its meaning: *(to ignore or hide something unpleasant or embarrassing.)*
Another volunteer leads a discuss session about the benefits of sharing difficulties.
*Examples:*
> *Venting emotions and receiving feedback from trustworthy people is therapeutic.*
> *Benefitting from another's experiences.*
> *Taking responsibility for mistakes eliminates the anxiety of being discovered.*

## Independent and Team Projects

### Independent
The pages as presented are independent projects.
Individuals identify a problem over which they had little control and journal about ways to reduce, reuse and recycle the issue.

### Team
Team members briefly formulate a scenario in which the main character faces adversity.
The opposing team(s) discuss:
> Factors over which the character did, or did not, have control.
> What the character could learn, gain, and do to help others.

### Individuals or Teams
Research teens, or fictional or historical characters, who triumphed over troubles.

**THOUGHT POWER** — Gifted and Talented Teens Workbook

# The Positive Realist

*Create a short story about three fictional teens who want the same outcome.*
*(Ex: a scholarship)*

**The characters:**
- An **illogical optimist** who believes the best will happen with little or no effort.
- A **pessimist** who expects the worst outcome regardless of any kind of effort.
- A **positive realist** who has an idea of what can be achieved with effort and perseverance.

Use this template:

| Illogical Optimist | Pessimist | Positive Realist |
|---|---|---|
| Fictional Character's Name | Fictional Character's Name | Fictional Character's Name |
| Same Desired Outcome | Same Desired Outcome | Same Desired Outcome |
| Fictional Character's Thoughts | Fictional Character's Thoughts | Fictional Character's Thoughts |
| Fictional Character's Actions or Non-Actions | Fictional Character's Actions or Non-Actions | Fictional Character's Actions or Non-Actions |
| Outcome | Outcome | Outcome |

# The Positive Realist - Facilitator Possibilities

## Strengths and Opportunities
Differentiate between pessimism, illogical optimism, and positive realism.

## Supplies
The Positive Realist handout and pens.

## Inquisitive Minds
Ask, "What does it mean to be called a *Pollyanna*?"
Elicit: To be like the literary character who was unreasonably optimistic.
Ask participants to briefly debate this idea: Believe and achieve.
Possibilities:
> Proponents may prioritize positive thinking over any obstacle.
> Opponents may emphasize external factors, personal effort, etc.

## Suggestions
Distribute The Positive Realist.
After completion, volunteers share their responses.

## Wrap-Up
Role play similar scenarios with the following characters:
> A teen who wants a specific outcome.
> Three friends: the illogical optimist, the pessimist, and the positive realist, who give advice that exemplifies their mindsets.
> The audience members discuss how the teen would be affected by following each type of advice.

## Independent and Team Projects
### Independent
The page as presented is an independent project.

### Team
Three teams each complete one of the three columns.
Each team reads aloud their character's description.
The other teams guess the outcomes.

### Individuals or Teams
Describe situations in which one has been illogically optimistic, pessimistic, and positively realistic.

# Artificial Intelligence: Versus Human Intelligence

Artificial intelligence like a GPS, voice activated speaker, search engines, and smart phones can research, answer questions, refer you to resources, and even respond: "That's okay" when you say: "I'm sorry."

**What do you think your human intelligence can do that a thinking machine cannot do?**

*(Ex: compromise)*

**In what ways can you put your human intelligence into action?**

*(Ex: resolve conflict)*

# Artificial Intelligence: Human Skills

Describe a specific situation in which you can use your
human intelligence for each of the following skills:

**Empathy**
*Feel someone's discomfort and respond to their thoughts and feelings.*

**Creative Problem Solving in a Group**
*Discuss an innovative idea with others.*

**Story Telling**
*Share a personal experience that listeners may choose to apply to their lives.*

**Persuasion**
*Motivate others to try a decision-making technique that has been helpful to you.*

**Creative Expression**
*Use poetry, art, music, or other methods to elicit an emotion.*

# Artificial Intelligence: Values

Humans hold values: beliefs and behavioral guidelines
about what is important, acceptable, ethical, etc.

*Create a collage illustrating your values using sketches, icons, words, phrases, images, words, photos, or pictures.*

Gifted and Talented Teens Workbook — **THOUGHT POWER**

# Artificial Intelligence – Facilitator Possibilities

**Strengths and Opportunities**
>Identify what one's human intelligence can do which artificial intelligence cannot do.

**Supplies**
>Handouts and pens.
>Optional: Art supplies for the *Values* collage.

**Inquisitive Minds**
>Ask, "What is artificial intelligence?
>>*A computer or machine that has been created to "think" and respond like a human.*
>Ask, "What is human intelligence?"
>>*A mental quality that consists of the abilities to learn from experience, adapt to new situations, understand and handle abstract concepts, and use knowledge to manipulate one's environment.*

**Suggestions**
>Distribute the first handout: ***Artificial Intelligence: Versus Human Intelligence,*** page 43.
>After completion, volunteers share their responses.
>Distribute ***Artificial Intelligence: Human Skills,*** page 44, and allow time for participants to briefly note their ideas, and then volunteers actually demonstrate aspects as follows:
>>1. Role-play the empathy situation.
>>2. Lead a group discussion.
>>3. Tell a personal experience and ask peers how they may apply it to their lives.
>>4. Present a persuasive decision-making technique and ask if peers plan to try it.
>>5. Share poetry, drawings, etc. and ask peers to describe the emotions they feel.
>
>Distribute ***Artificial Intelligence: Values***, page 45.
>After completion, volunteers share their responses..

**Wrap-Up**
>Participants form two teams who briefly meet in different areas of the room.
>Each team makes notes to argue "No" or "Yes" to this question:
>>*Will artificial intelligence take over the world?*
>Teams debate and provide rebuttals and closing arguments for a specified length of time.

**Independent and Team Projects**
>**Independent**
>>The pages as presented are independent projects.
>
>**Team**
>>***Artificial Intelligence: Human Skills,*** page 44, can be completed by five teams.
>>Each team completes a different aspect of human intelligence then shares with the group.
>
>**Individuals or Teams**
>>Select one's area of interest: science, politics, medical advances, transportation, robotics, the military, etc.
>>Research ways artificial intelligence is impacting that field.

# Reprogram Your Irrational Thoughts

Irrational = not based in reason or logic

Imagine that your computerized personal assistant, named Re-Pro, can reprogram your irrational thoughts.

*Ex:* **You,** "Re-Pro … I have to please others to feel good about myself."
**Re-Pro,** "You have to act according to your values to feel good about yourself."
**You,** "Re-pro … If I make a mistake, I'm a failure."
**Re-Pro,** "If you make a mistake, you learn what not to do."

*Re-program the following thoughts by writing Re-Pro's responses.*

**Person:** "Re-Pro …I don't deserve success."

**Re-Pro,** "_____"


**Person:** "Re-Pro … I must fulfill someone else's dream for my future."

**Re-Pro,** "_____"


**Person:** "Re-Pro …If I try something difficult and don't do it well, I'll feel like a failure."

**Re-Pro,** "_____"


**Person:** "Re-Pro …If I succeed at this, they'll expect me to do even more and I might let them down."

**Re-Pro,** "_____"

Reprogram your irrational thoughts by writing your thoughts and Re-Pro's responses.

**You:** "Re-Pro "_____"

**Re-Pro,** "_____"


**You:** "Re-Pro "_____"

**Re-Pro,** "_____"


**You:** "Re-Pro "_____"

**Re-Pro,** "_____"

# Reprogram Your Irrational Thoughts - Facilitator Possibilities

**Strengths and Opportunities**
    Recognize and replace irrational thoughts.

**Supplies**
    Reprogram Your Irrational Thoughts handout and pens.
    Board and marker.

**Inquisitive Minds**
    Ask, "What tasks do you ask your computerized personal assistant to perform?"
    Ask, "What would you think about a computerized assistant that argues with you?"

**Suggestions**
    Distribute the Reprogram Your Irrational Thoughts handout.
    After completion, volunteers share their responses.

**Wrap-Up**
    *Write the following irrational thoughts on the board and elicit arguments against them.*
    "If I do something for myself, it means I'm selfish."
    "I lose my temper because people provoke me."
    "When I'm criticized, it means I'm a loser."
    "If I give an opinion that differs from other people's opinions, they will dislike me."

**Independent and Team Projects**
    **Independent**
        The page as presented is an independent project.
    **Team**
        Teams compose lists of irrational thoughts.
        Team members form two parallel rows, facing each other.
        The list is passed down each row as team members take turns reading a thought to the other team's member sitting or standing opposite them.
        The opposing team members argue against the irrational thoughts.

    **Individuals or Teams**
        Individuals or the whole group theorize the origin of irrational thoughts.
            *Possibilities:*
            Erroneous comments by others that one has internalized; social media pressure to be liked, perfectionism, role models who obsess about what people think about them, etc.

# What Do You Think About Stress? EUSTRESS

People often think that all stress is unpleasant, however,
there are different types of stress.

<u>Eustress</u> is a moderate stress: beneficial and positive.
It feels exciting, focuses energy, motivates, is short-term, and improves performance.
*Ex: An exciting, challenging work assignment that is
perceived to be neither too difficult nor too easy.*

*Think about a time you have felt stressed and excited at the same time.
Describe or draw an example of how you felt
when you experienced this eustress.*

# What Do You Think About Stress? DISTRESS

People know that distress feels terrible, and
it can accompany upsetting experiences.

<u>Distress</u> **causes concern, feels unpleasant, is often extreme, and diminishes performance.
Distress stems from fear, repetitive negative thoughts, and unrealistic perfectionism.**
*Ex: money, sleep, abuse issues, death, break up, conflicts, fear of failure, etc.*

*Stream of conscious writing mimics thoughts and flows like a stream or river.
Write in an unstructured, unedited way, about your experiences with distress.
You can write around the edges, in circles, in squiggles, or any pattern.*

# What Do You Think About Stress? BUTTERFLIES

All *butterflies* in your stomach are not alike.

Butterflies stem from the fight or flight response which decreases blood flow to the stomach and increases blood flow to muscles. Butterflies can be two-sided: One side signifies opportunity, and the other side signifies danger or disappointment. The outcome is unknown.

*Ex: A new relationship that could bloom or break up.*

**A poem may have any rhyme pattern, or it may not rhyme.**

*Example:*
> Unsure
> I'm riding the wave with us on my mind.
> I'm hoping that we will find
> That we can be sure our love will endure,
> And no one is left behind.
> **~ Carol Butler Cooper**

*Do you think the teen would take the risk of entering this relationship?* _____

Explain _____

*Write your poem about a character whose butterflies could mean opportunity on one side and danger or disappointment on the other side.*

Title _____

_____

_____

_____

_____

_____

Would your character take this risk? _____ Explain:

_____

_____

_____

_____

_____

*Gifted and Talented Teens Workbook* — **THOUGHT POWER**

# What Do You Think About Stress? – Facilitator Possibilities

### Strengths and Opportunities
Explore the effects of eustress and distress.

### Supplies
Four What Do You Think About Stress handouts and pens.
Optional: Art supplies.

### Inquisitive Minds
Ask, "What do you think about stress?"
"What situations can result in stress?"

### Suggestions
Distribute the four handouts.
After completion, volunteers share their responses.

### Wrap-Up
Promote a discussion about the benefits of *fight, flight,* or *freeze* responses in danger.
Promote a discussion about the drawbacks of *fight, flight,* or *freeze* in healthy risk situations.
Elicit examples of butterflies in the stomach that warn that a relationship could be dangerous.
Elicit that if one avoids risk, disappointment might not happen, but positive outcomes are also precluded.

### Independent and Team Projects

**Independent**
The pages as presented are independent projects.

**Team**
Two of the pages can be used as a bulletin board or poster project by teams or the group:
What Do You Think About Stress? Eustress? and *Butterflies?*
Participants put their illustrations and poems on the board.

**Individuals or Teams**
Individuals journal or teams brainstorm situations in which …
They took a healthy risk, the outcome, and what was gained by the experience.
They did not take a healthy risk, whether they regret their inaction, and why.

# Shedding Light on the Subject

*Personalize these idioms regarding light.*

*Light – understanding and awareness of a problem or a mystery.*

I wish I could see the light about _____ .

I stand in my own light when _____ .

I am giving myself the green light to _____ .

I am slowing down for a yellow light regarding _____ .

I am beginning to see _____ in a whole new light.

I would like to shed some light on _____ .

I had a lightbulb moment when _____ .

My guiding light is _____ .

The light of my life is _____ .

I hide my own light when _____ .

I need to light a fire under myself regarding _____ .

I can be a beam of light in this situation _____ .

I hope to see the light at the end of the tunnel regarding _____ .

I can be a leading light for _____ .

Maybe it would help to make light of _____ .

People need to lighten up on me regarding _____ .

It may help if I tread lightly on _____ .

I can shine my light by _____ .

*In the box below, compose you own idiom about light.*

# Shedding Light on the Subject - Facilitator Possibilities

**Strengths and Opportunities**
Explore the aspects of LIGHT in one's life in the following context:
*"Understanding and awareness of a problem or a mystery."*

**Supplies**
Shedding the Light handout and pens.
Art supplies.

**Inquisitive Minds**
Ask, "What does it mean to shed light on something?"
Volunteers share stories about times they helped others to understand an issue.

**Suggestions**
Distribute *Shedding the Light* handout.
After completion, volunteers share their responses.

**Wrap-Up**
Participants draw or use symbols to represent an idiom that has special meaning to them.
Reassure participants they may keep their work private.
Volunteers may choose to play the *Guess My Idiom* game.
Volunteers take turns showing their representations. Participants guess the idiom represented.
Volunteers may share insights they developed through the process.

**Independent and Team Projects**
**Independent**
The page as presented is an independent project.
Individuals may choose an idiom and journal about its personal relevance.
**Team**
Teams research idioms on self-selected topics and apply them to their lives.

**Individuals or Teams**
Individuals or teams create their own idioms about self-selected topics.
Individuals journal and teams discuss ways the idioms apply to their lives.

# Your Mind's Lens – Close-Up

Your perspective depends on your mind's lens.
Some issues require close-up examination.

Take a close-up selfie of your thoughts and feelings about a personal issue.
Express your close-up selfie visually and/or verbally.

*Gifted and Talented Teens Workbook* — **THOUGHT POWER**

# Your Mind's Lens – Panorama

In panorama views, an ultra-wide angle
connects a series of adjacent shots.

*Express adjacent shots about your issue on the
Close-Up page, pictorially or verbally.*
*Ex: Adjacent shots may include timelines, your past that colors your present view, factors outside yourself, intuitions, trusted people's opinions, pros and cons, hopes, beliefs, etc.*

My Issue

_____
_____

My Adjacent Shots

|  |  |  |  |
|---|---|---|---|
|  |  |  |  |
|  |  |  |  |
|  |  |  |  |

Thinking about the big picture of this issue, I may decide to _____
_____
_____

# Your Mind's Lens – Magnify, Minimize, or Use Tunnel Vision?

*Small stuff that I tend to magnify into a big deal:*

1. _____
2. _____
3. _____
4. _____
5. _____

*Big stuff that I tend to minimize by denying or overlooking:*

1. _____
2. _____
3. _____
4. _____
5. _____

*Examples of tunnel vision, where I tend to focus excessively on one point of view.*

1. _____
2. _____
3. _____
4. _____
5. _____

I may decide to adjust my view by _____

_____

_____

# Your Mind's Lens - Facilitator Possibilities

**Strengths and Opportunities**
    Recognize the value of a *close-up* and of a *panoramic* view of one's life.

**Supplies**
    Three *Your Mind's Lens* handouts and pens.
    Art supplies.

**Inquisitive Minds**
    Ask, "What are your favorite features of your cell phones?"
    Encourage a brief discussion about cell phone cameras.

**Suggestions**
    Distribute the three Your Mind's Lens handouts.
    After completion, volunteers share their responses.

**Wrap-Up**
    Ask, "What do people's photos reveal about their lives?"
    Encourage a discussion about photos that show priorities, preferences, social life, and percentage of selfies versus photos of others, etc.

**Independent and Team Projects**
    **Independent**
        The pages as presented are independent projects.
    **Team**
        Teams collaborate to create other analogies related to photos and the mind's lens.
            *Ex: lack of depth, poor lighting, blurry pictures, over-exposure, cluttered background, lack of breathing space around the subject of the photo, etc.*

    **Individuals or Teams**
        Individuals journal about, or teams discuss, the personal implications of one of the examples noted in the Team suggestions above.

# Your Values Indicator

An aircraft's *altitude indicator* is an instrument that shows the aircraft's orientation relative to the earth's horizon – whether it is maintaining, ascending, descending, or turning.

Imagine that you have a *values indicator* that shows your actions relative to your values.

***Describe a value you are maintaining.*** *(To keep or continue as is.)* _____
_____
_____

What are the ways you are doing this? _____
_____

***Describe a value you are ascending from.*** *(Rising above and beyond.)* _____
_____
_____

What are the ways you are doing this? _____
_____
_____

***Describe a value you are descending from.*** *(Behaving below your expectations.)* _____
_____
_____

What are the ways you are doing this? _____
_____
_____

***Describe a value you are tempted to turn away from.*** _____
_____

*How could that cause you to crash?* _____
_____

# Your Values Indicator – Facilitator Possibilities

**Strengths and Opportunities**
    Identify personal values.
    Identify conditions that lead to maintaining, ascending, or turning away from one's values.

**Supplies**
    Your Values Indicator handout and pens.

**Inquisitive Minds**
    Ask, "What are values?"
        *(Values are a person's principles or standards of behaviors.*
        *One's judgment of what is important in life.)*
    Encourage participants to brainstorm a list of personal values.

**Suggestions**
    Distribute the Your Values handout.
    After completion, volunteers share their responses.

**Wrap-Up**
    Elicit that pilots find instruments particularly important in weather that causes poor visibility.
    Ask, "What could cloud a person's ability to stick to personal values?"
    A volunteer leads a discussion session and lists participants' ideas.
      Possibilities:
        Wanting an outcome regardless of personal values.
        Pressure from peers, families, society, media, social media, etc.
        Liking someone so much that one ignores personal values.
        Wanting to be a part of a group and going along with them no matter what.
        Substances that alter one's mind and mood.

**Independent and Team Projects**
  **Independent**
      The page as presented is an independent project.
  **Team**
      Teams select a value to portray via improv theater.
      The main character is tempted to descend or turn away from that value.
      The audience yells out ways to maintain and ascend above the value.

  **Individuals or Teams**
      Research science fiction heroes' and role models' biographies to identify
          examples of maintaining and ascending above personal values, despite
          temptations to descend or turn away … or not.

CHAPTER 3

# Giving Back

Giving back means using your gifts, talents, experiences, beliefs, time, energy, and money or material goods, to improve the world close to home (family, friends, school, and community) and further away (your country and the world.) When you advocate for a person or a cause close to your heart, you feel almost as gratified as those who receive your help.

Giving back positively impacts your life. Your gifts and talents thrive when you use them for a compassionate purpose. You can meet like-minded people, become part of a productive team, access leadership opportunities, share your knowledge, and develop or improve your skills.

> It's a no-fail, incontrovertible reality:
> If you get, give. If you learn, teach.
> You can't do anything with that except do it.
> ~ **Maya Angelou**

In this chapter teens acknowledge that disagreements can lead to innovation, and conflict can be resolved. Teens apply sportsmanship concepts to sports and other competitive situations and identify ways to manage wins, losses, and mistakes. Teens practice communication, leadership, and followership.

**GIVING BACK** — Gifted and Talented Teens Workbook

# Re-Gift

Identify one of your gifts or talents.
Creatively express ways you can re-gift your intangible quality – a gift from your heart!

# Re-Gift - Facilitator Possibilities

**Strengths and Opportunities**
　　Recognize ways to re-gift one's positive traits to friends, family, school, community, and society.

**Supplies**
　　Re-Gift handout, pens, and optional:
　　　　Board, markers, paper, colored pencils, or other art supplies.
　　Access to the Internet for research.

**Inquisitive Minds**
　　Before the activity, recruit a participant to ask the following question and listen to the responses.
　　"What are the pros and cons of re-gifting holiday or birthday gifts?"

**Suggestions**
　　Prompt a discussion of intangible gifts and talents including character traits of compassion, etc.
　　Distribute the Re-Gift handout and supplies.
　　Suggest that participants may draw, use symbols, write prose or poetry, plan a role-play, compose lyrics, etc., to show ways to give back to people who are close to them and to society.
　　After completion, volunteers share their work.

**Wrap-Up**
　　Elicit some differences between re-gifting tangible and intangible gifts.
　　　*Examples:*
　　　*Tangible Gifts – can be unwanted or gone forever.*
　　　*Intangible Gifts – are valued and appreciated the more they are shared.*

**Independent and Team Projects**
　　**Independent**
　　　　Participants list their own personal gifts and talents, and note ways to re-gift.

　　**Team**
　　　　　Divide the group into two teams.
　　　　　　　Teams each discuss and make a list of gifts and talents.
　　　　　　　Teams then identify ways to re-gift the other teams' list of gifts and talents.

　　**Individuals or Teams**
　　　　Research and share ways teens have used gifts and talents to benefit others.

GIVING BACK — Gifted and Talented Teens Workbook

# HELP IS ON THE WAY!

Cut out the boxes below.
On the back of each box, write a situation in which that person needs help.

| Sibling | Parent/caregiver | Elderly relative | Friend | Co-worker |
|---|---|---|---|---|
| Classmate | Teammate | Club member | Teacher | Supervisor |
| Newcomer | Person dealing with a problem | A younger person | Elderly neighbor | Other |

*Gifted and Talented Teens Workbook* — **GIVING BACK**

# HELP IS ON THE WAY! – Facilitator Possibilities

**Strengths and Opportunities**
   Identify ways to help others.

**Supplies**
   Scissors for the facilitator to cut out the boxes on the handout.
   Guess my Trait handout and pens for independent projects.

**Inquisitive Minds**
   Ask, "Have you ever had the impulse to help someone, then talked yourself out of it?"
      (Encourage volunteers to elaborate).

**Suggestions**
   Distribute the Help is on the Way handout.
   Participants read the text, cut out the boxes, write on the backs, and stack their cutouts.
   Everyone's cutouts are collected, shuffled, and placed in a stack at the front of the room.
   Participants take turns picking up a cutout, reading the front (person) and back (situation) aloud.
   Volunteers provide feedback regarding ACT, THINK, and PLAN possibilities.

**Wrap-Up**
   Participants discuss ways to go beyond individual helping – ways to alleviate or prevent the problems with the family, at school, in the community, or with social media.
      *Ex: Make a list of community resources to insert into food bags for people who are homeless.*

**Independent and Team Projects**
   **Independent**
      The handout remains uncut.
      Individuals select one or more of the people named on the front, and describe on the back:
         SITUATION and ACT, THINK, and/or PLAN options.

   **Team**
      Participants identify a group of people who need help, e.g., people who are bullied.
      Teams (Home, School, Community, and Social Media) conceptualize ways to help.

   **Individuals or Teams**
      Individuals journal, and teams discuss stories of times they needed help and how others responded re: ACT, THINK, and PLAN.

GIVING BACK — Gifted and Talented Teens Workbook

# Talents Used for a Cause — TALENTS

**Talent** – a natural aptitude or skill. Example: art, technology, sports.

*Write as many talents as possible next to the appropriate starting letters.
(It is not necessary to fill in each of the letters.)
Highlight the TALENTS most descriptive of you.*

| | | | |
|---|---|---|---|
| A | | N | |
| B | | O | |
| C | | P | |
| D | | Q | |
| E | | R | |
| F | | S | |
| G | | T | |
| H | | U | |
| I | | V | |
| J | | W | |
| K | | X | |
| L | | Y | |
| M | | Z | |

# Talents Used for a Cause

**CAUSE** - an aim or principle one commits to defend or advocate. *Ex: human rights, animals.*

Write as many possible causes next to the appropriate starting letters.
*(It is not necessary to fill in each of the letters.)*
Highlight the CAUSES most important to you where you could use your TALENTS.

| | | | |
|---|---|---|---|
| A | | N | |
| B | | O | |
| C | | P | |
| D | | Q | |
| E | | R | |
| F | | S | |
| G | | T | |
| H | | U | |
| I | | V | |
| J | | W | |
| K | | X | |
| L | | Y | |
| M | | Z | |

# Talents Used for a Cause — COMBINATIONS

*Consider this true-to-life example:*

A photographer helps sick kids see themselves as superheroes by providing costumes, backdrops, and snapshots. His artistry brightens their days, and promotes images of strength to fight their diseases.

*Look again at your highlighted talents and causes.
In the thought cloud, dream up ways to combine
your talents with causes you care about.*

# Talents Used for a Cause: – Facilitator Possibilities

**Strengths and Opportunities**
Identify one's talents and ways to use them.

**Supplies**
Talents Used for a Cause - Combinations handout and pens; highlighters, board, and markers for the Team activity.

**Inquisitive Minds**
Ask, "What are the benefits of having gifts and talents?"
Ask, "What are the drawbacks of having gifts and talents?"

**Suggestions**
Distribute the Talents Used for a Cause - Combinations handout.
Participants read, follow the instructions, and complete the thought clouds.
Volunteers share their responses.

**Wrap-Up**
Participants identify one or more steps to take within the next month to support their causes.

**Independent and Team Projects**
**Independent**
The activity as presented is an independent activity

**Team**
Participants form two teams: The TALENTS, and The CAUSES.
The TALENTS elect a recorder who lists their ideas alphabetically on the TALENTS page.
The CAUSES (for example, clean water) elect a recorder who lists their ideas alphabetically on the CAUSES page
**The group reconvenes.**
A TALENT team member writes any talent from the list onto the board.
A CAUSE team member writes any cause on the board.
The group brainstorms ways to use that talent to promote that cause.
The process is repeated with other talents and causes.

**Individuals or Teams**
Create a cartoon or short story of a non-human superhero that uses a special talent to better the world.

# From Adversity to Advocacy

*A True-to-Life Example*

**Person's Situation**
Mr. X is a sentenced to a long prison term for several big bank robberies.

**Person's Challenges**
Mr. X has a history of alcohol and drug addiction. He also has limited job skills.

**Cost of Not Finding a Solution**
Mr. X could rotate in and out of prison without becoming sober or skilled.

**Mr. X's Solution**
Mr. X reads law books, develops a passion for the law, and helps other inmates appeal their cases.

**Mr. X's Results**
Upon release, Mr. X completes his law degree, is admitted to the bar association, and becomes a law professor at a prestigious university. He starts an organization that helps inmates turn their lives around through vocational training, mental health counseling, and substance abuse recovery.

*Create your true-to-life example about a person who turns adversity into advocacy.*

Person's Situation: _____
_____
_____

Person's Challenges: _____
_____
_____

Cost of Not Finding a Solution: _____
_____
_____

Person's Solution: _____
_____
_____

Person's Results: _____
_____
_____

# From Adversity to Advocacy: – Facilitator Possibilities

**Strengths and Opportunities**
    Recognize ways to use personal adversity to advocate for others with similar problems.

**Supplies**
    Adversity to Advocacy handout and pens.

**Inquisitive Minds**
    Ask, "What is adversity?" *(difficulties, misfortune, hardships, trouble, etc.)*
    Ask, "How can anything positive result from adversity?"

**Suggestions**
    Distribute the Adversity to Advocacy handout.
    After completion, volunteers share their case studies.

**Wrap-Up**
    Participants brainstorm ways people can turn triumphs into advocacy.
      *Ex: A champion boxer gives free boxing lessons at a local teen center.*

**Independent and Team Projects**
    **Independent**
        The activity as presented is an independent activity.
    **Team**
        Teams create true-to-life examples and present them to the group.

    **Individuals or Teams**
        Research people who have turned adversity or triumphs into advocacy in the arts, athletics, politics, etc.
        Volunteers share their findings.
        Send thoughts in a letter to someone who might benefit.

# Philanthropy Fantasy

**Pretend that you and your team have one million dollars.**
*Your team decides to begin a human services organization that will alleviate suffering, help solve underlying problems, and improve quality of life.*

**You will need a Mission Statement**
*It states the purpose of your organization, whom you will help, and the ways you will help.
The best mission statements are twenty words or less.*

*Ex: The Make-A-Wish Foundation: We grant the wishes of children with life-threatening medical conditions to enrich the human experience with hope, strength, and joy.*

1. Name your organization and write the Mission Statement.

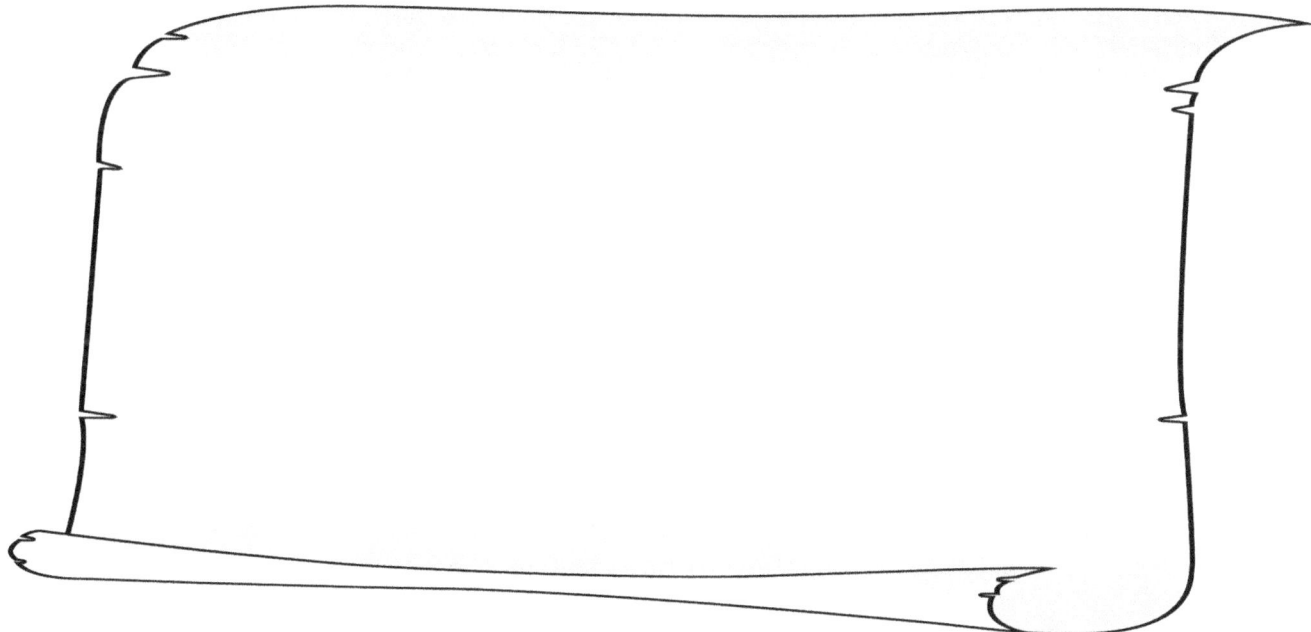

2. Copy your Mission Statement onto a poster board and attach it to your team's wall.
3. Copy each of these headings onto its own poster board and attach them to your team's wall.
   - Research
   - Fundraising
   - Community outreach
   - Multi-media campaign
   - Like-minded employees and volunteers
4. Pretend that it is now your five-year anniversary.
   Create one client's success story that came about because of your organization's efforts.

_____
_____
_____
_____

# Philanthropy Fantasy: – Facilitator Possibilities

**Strengths and Opportunities**
    Empower one to make a positive difference in other people's lives.

**Supplies**
    Philanthropy Fantasy handout and pens; poster board or large paper; tape and markers.

**Inquisitive Minds**
    Ask, "What would you do with a million dollars?"

**Suggestions**
    Depending on the number of participants and wall or board space, create teams.
    Each team needs six pieces of poster board or large paper and tape.
    Teams occupy a portion of wall or board space, which is their station.
    Distribute Philanthropy Fantasy handout.
    Each team will follow these steps:
        Brainstorm and agree on a different segment of the population to serve.
        Post their mission statement and prepare poster boards with the headings.
        Creates their client's success story and writes it on one member's handout.
    Participants from all teams will follow these steps:
        Circulate through their own and other teams' stations.
        Add ideas under each team's five poster board headings.
        Return to stations.

**Wrap-Up**
    Team members from each station present their *Philanthropy Fantasy* by reading their mission statement, the ideas on the poster board paper, and their client's story aloud.

**Independent and Team Projects**
    **Independent**
        Journal responses to Numbers 1 and 4 on the front of the handout.
        Copy the Number 3 headings onto the back of the handout and list ideas.
    **Team**
        The page as presented is a team activity.
        Teams discuss ways to make their philanthropy fantasy a reality.

    **Individuals or Teams**
        Research human services organizations that have been started by teens.

# Promote Your Platform

A platform can be a set of beliefs or a declared policy.

Politicians, sports stars, celebrities, and anyone on social media often have a platform.
Your platform can open people's minds and touch their hearts.
The beliefs you try to live by can be food-for-thought for your followers.

**Name a celebrity who has a platform which you respect.**

_____

**What is this person's platform?**

_____
_____
_____

Write or draw YOUR platform.

# Promote Your Platform – Facilitator Possibilities

**Strengths and Opportunities**
    Recognize one's personal beliefs and take a stand.

**Supplies**
    Promote Your Platform handout and pens.

**Inquisitive Minds**
    Ask, "What is a political party platform?"
    Request: "Give examples of people who are not politicians who promote a platform."
        *Ex: An actor endorsing eco-activism; sports teams speaking out against domestic violence.*

**Suggestions**
    Distribute the Promote Your Platform handout, elicit ground rules for platforms.
        *(Platforms need to be honest, positive. Platforms should not put down others or promote exclusion, etc.).*
    After completion, volunteers share their platforms.
    Peers jot down platforms they want to adopt.

**Wrap-Up**
    Participants are encouraged to post their positive and helpful platforms on social media.

**Independent and Team Projects**
    **Independent**
        The page as presented is an independent activity.
    **Team**
        Teams select different segments to represent via platforms.
        *Possibilities:*
        Sports stars may promote teamwork, being humble winners, and learning from losses.
        Musicians may promote inspiring lyrics and/or social justice messages.
        Actors may promote documentaries and thought-provoking movies.

    **Individuals or Teams**
        Individuals or teams research platforms of role models, celebrities, or athletes.
        Teams research different political party platforms and debate their pros and cons.

# Gratitude Gives

*Gratitude fosters reciprocity, giving back what was received.*

*Gratitude encourages pro-social behavior that is productive, positive, and beneficial to society.*

*Finish the sentences to describe your gratitude through reciprocal and prosocial behaviors.*

*Example:*
*I am grateful to my teachers for* sticking with me when I just didn't get it.
*I can give back by* tutoring other kids.

I am grateful to my teachers for _____

I can give back by _____


I am grateful to my friends for_____

I can give back by _____


I am grateful to my parents/caregivers for _____

I can give back by _____


I am grateful to my coach, band-leader, or other mentors for _____

I can give back by _____


I am grateful to _____ for _____

I can give back by _____


I am grateful for the ability to _____

I can use it productively by_____


I am grateful for my belief that _____

I can share it with others by _____


I am grateful for my value of _____

I can use it to benefit others by _____

# Gratitude Gives – Facilitator Possibilities

**Strengths and Opportunities**
    Identify ways to express gratitude through reciprocal and pro-social behaviors.

**Supplies**
    Gratitude Gives handout and pens.

**Inquisitive Minds**
    Ask, "In what ways do people express gratitude?"
    Ask for examples of people who have been grateful even when facing difficulties.
        *(Survivors of disasters who lose all their material belongings are grateful to be alive.)*

**Suggestions**
    Distribute the Gratitude Gives handout.
    After completion, volunteers share their responses.

**Wrap-Up**
    Have a Reciprocity Bee.
        Participants stand in a circle and take turns as follows:
        A volunteer shares a story about someone who showed him/her kindness.
        Each peer states a way to give back gratitude until someone cannot come up with another idea.
        The person who cannot add an idea sits.
        The next person states a new story about a kindness received.
        Peers add ways to give back gratitude until someone cannot, and he or she sits.
        They play until one person is left standing.

**Independent and Team Projects**
    **Independent**
        The page as presented is an independent activity.
    **Team**
        Teams select a gift, list ways to give back to society, and then share with the group.
        Possible gifts: Intelligent, compassionate, open-minded, creative, innovative, persevering, etc.

    **Individuals or Teams**
        Research the impact of gratitude on willingness to give back, positive perspective, etc.
        Individuals journal and teams share ways others have shown gratitude to them.

# Where Does Your Money Go?

Your money may be funding a business practice or charity to which you might not want to contribute. You might speak out against it if you knew more about it!

*TEAM 1: You can find out about what your money actually funds. It could fund exploitation of humans or it can operate with strict fair labor practices.*
   *Examples:  Some chocolate, clothing, shoes, electronics, etc., are made in prison-like conditions for little pay, by adult forced labor or by children stolen from their homes.*
*Socially conscious companies pay fairly, and provide healthy and fair working conditions.*
   *REPORTERS will present an exposé about these companies:*

| Child Labor or Forced Labor Company and Its Products | Alternative Fair Labor Company and Its Similar Products |
|---|---|
| Notes | Notes |

*TEAM 2: You could choose to buy from businesses with a sense of responsibility for people in need.*
   *Example:   a company buys a pair of eyeglasses for someone in need for each pair of glasses they sell. ADVERTISERS will produce a commercial:*

| A Company that Gives Back and Their Products | Ways the Company Gives Back |
|---|---|
| Notes | Notes |

*TEAM 3: You could choose to use your voice and your money as an entrepreneur who improves lives.*
   *Example:   A seventeen-year-old builds a drone to explore dangerous environments to help first responders find trapped people.*
ENTREPRENEURS will research and imagine, and then describe an entrepreneur's product.

| An Entrepreneur Whose Product Improves Life or Safety | An Imagined Entrepreneur Whose Product Improves Life or Safety |
|---|---|
| Notes | Notes |

# Where Does Your Money Go? – Facilitator Possibilities

### Strengths and Opportunities
Recognize ways to align one's expenditures with one's values.

### Supplies
Where Does Your Money Go handout and pens, cell phone, and other items to show
  for Inquisitive Minds below.
Optional for teams to create their medical reports, commercials, or product:
  Art supplies, printer for photos, table and chairs if journalists want a panel discussion.

### Inquisitive Minds
Show: A cell phone, piece of chocolate, shoe, and a garment.
Ask, "What do these items potentially have in common?" *(Possibly made by slave labor)*.

### Suggestions
Distribute the Where Does Your Money Go handout.
Participants read silently, and decide on their team: Journalists, Advertisers, or Entrepreneurs.
Team members research and create their investigative report, commercial, or new product.

### Wrap-Up
The group re-convenes and teams present their report, commercial, or product.
Participants from other teams provide feedback and discuss the issue.

### Independent and Team Projects
#### Independent
The page can be completed by individuals who choose one of the three options, or all three options. Volunteers present their reports, commercials, or new products.
#### Team
The page as presented is a team activity.

#### Individuals or Teams
Create dilemma questions to ask peers.
*Ex: Your small business is barely breaking even. You could make your product cheaply offshore using forced labor, or lose your profit margin by employing workers in your country for a fair wage. What do you do and why?*

# FORGIVENESS: The Gift that Gives Back

## Questions for Discussion:

1. Why do you think people are advised to forgive?
2. Does forgiving mean forgetting? Why or Why not?
3. Would you forgive someone who has not apologized? Why or why not?
4. Does forgiveness give the person a right to continue the behavior? Why or why not?
5. How could you forgive someone who broke the law?
6. What wrongs do you believe are unforgivable? Why?
7. Would you forgive someone who is clueless about hurting you? Why or why not?
8. Would you forgive a person who is no longer a part of your life? Why or why not?
9. Do you have to say "I forgive you" to a person? Why or why not?
10. What does forgiveness mean to the continuing of a relationship?
11. Does forgiveness mean you keep abuse a secret? Why or why not?
12. With whom would you discuss abuse? Why?
13. In the long run, how does it feel to get revenge?
14. Is forgiveness a feeling or a decision? Explain.
15. What would you do if resentment caused emotional pain?
16. How does holding a grudge hurt a person?
17. How does holding a grudge affect you?
18. In what ways can refusal to forgive make a person feel like a victim?
19. How does a person free oneself from the victim role?
20. How can forgiveness be a gift that gives back to you?

# FORGIVENESS: The Gift that Gives Back - Facilitator Possibilities

**Strengths and Opportunities**
Identify ways to forgive oneself and forgive others.

**Supplies**
Forgiveness: The Gift That Gives Back handout and pens.

**Inquisitive Minds**
Ask, "What do you think are some gifts that come back to you?"

**Suggestions**
Photocopy enough handouts for all participants but keep one master copy initially.
Explain that the responses are to be personal opinions; no response will be labeled wrong.
A questioner asks the first four questions and elicits as many peer responses as possible.
The next questioners continue until all twenty questions have been addressed.
At the end, if the participants have not made the following points, elicit these concepts:
1. Forgiveness is for us, not the other person and we all need to be forgiven at times.
2. You might not forget; the memory may help you to avoid further situations like this.
3. You may never receive an apology.
4. You can set boundaries of what will not be tolerated or you can end the relationship.
5. Forgive, but tell law enforcement and others who will protect the public and seek justice.
6. No wrongs are unforgivable because forgiving sets the survivor free.
7. Yes, some may never acknowledge hurting you; they may not realize they hurt you.
8. Yes, you forgive for your own peace of mind.
9. No! Your will to forgive is what matters.
10. If it's worth saving, and it isn't toxic, forgiveness will help restoration.
11. Never keep it a secret; report abuse.
12. Talk with a parent/caregiver, trusted adult, teacher, counselor, or the police. These people can help.
13. Not in the long run; regret and guilt follow. Two wrongs don't make a right.
14. A decision: you may not feel like it but you can decide to forgive for your own peace of mind.
15. Pain means something is wrong; if resentment causes emotional pain, let it go!
16. Holding a grudge does not hurt the person who hurt you; it hurts you.
17. Grudges lead to lingering anger, hurt, self-pity, and possibly desire for revenge, depression, etc.
18. You empower the person who hurt you to keep you stuck in your anger and misery.
19. You forgive; set boundaries if the relationship continues; access counseling or legal help if needed.
20. You give yourself relief from resentment, motivation to move forward; you gain wisdom.

Distribute Forgiveness: The Gift That Gives Back handout to all participants to journal about applicable questions for homework.

**Wrap-Up**
Encourage a discussion about the difficulty, benefits, and ways to forgive oneself.

**Independent and Team Projects**

**Independent**
Individuals journal responses.

**Team**
Moderators ask, panelists respond, and the audience adds to their opinions.

**Individuals or Teams**
Individuals journal and teams tell stories about times they needed forgiveness, whether it was given or withheld, and their related feelings.

# Use Idioms to Give Back

*Ask your partner the questions below, write the partner's responses; then switch roles.*
*HAVE FUN WITH THESE ITALICIZED IDIOMS!*

Identify your *Achilles heel*. How can you help others with similar vulnerabilities? _____
_____
_____

What *eye-opener* changed your outlook on a certain person whom you would like to help? _____
_____
_____

Discuss an issue you *cannot stomach* that you can *rack your brain* to improve. _____
_____
_____

In what ways can your *gift of gab* help improve a situation? _____
_____
_____

State a *ground rule* that you live by. In what ways can you encourage others to consider this rule?
_____
_____

Who could benefit from a *pat on the back* from you? How can you do this? _____
_____
_____

What cause needs your *elbow grease*? How can you *roll up your sleeves* to help? _____
_____
_____

About what issue have you *held your tongue* too long? How will you *stick your neck out* to help? _____
_____
_____

Describe your *gut feeling* that tells you your *heart is in the right place* about giving back. _____
_____
_____

# Use Idioms to Give Back - Facilitator Possibilities

**Strengths and Opportunities**
   Acknowledge insights about giving back.

**Supplies**
   Ask, "Give examples of problems you could see, hear about, and smell, that you could take action to improve."
   Possibilities:
      See a student sitting alone at lunch time; sit with the person.
      Hear that neighbors lost belongings in a fire; take up a collection of items they need.
      Smell an unwashed odor on some people who are homeless; hand out hygiene supplies.

**Inquisitive Minds**
   Ask, "What is rapport?" and "When do you need to develop rapport with people?"

**Suggestions**
   Divide the group into partners.
   Distribute the Idioms to Give Back handout to all.
   Partners follow the directions on the handout and may write on the back if necessary.
   If participants are unfamiliar with an idiom, encourage unique interpretations, or they may look up *Idioms about Body Parts*. Volunteers share their own responses with the group.

**Wrap-Up**
   Participants imagine or look up idioms about giving back and write related questions.
   Participants read their questions aloud and volunteers respond.

**Independent and Team Projects**
   **Independent**
      Individuals journal responses.
   **Team**
      Each team addresses one idiom and deliberates responses for ten minutes.
      The group re-convenes, and teams share their responses.

   **Individuals or Teams**
      Create a short story about a character who exemplifies any idiom related to giving back.

CHAPTER 4

# TEAM PLAYER

> Gifted and talented teens often rise to leadership roles, but sometimes being a team player is equally important. Teamwork is a cooperative, coordinated effort of two or more people working together toward a common purpose. When we think of teams, we often think of sports. However, teams exist in homes, classrooms, clubs, groups of friends, workplaces, community organizations, and many other settings.
>
> Effective team players respect and depend on each other, discuss issues, solve problems, resolve conflicts, and share each other's challenges and triumphs.

*None of us is as smart as all of us.*
*~ Ken Blanchard*

---

In this chapter teens share ideas about topics important to them through their choices of visual art, the written or spoken word, theater, dance, music, fantasy, and other techniques. Teens change self-limiting thoughts into personal power, identify insights, evoke emotions, and take healthy risks through creative expression.

**TEAM PLAYER** — Gifted and Talented Teens Workbook

# AGREE TO DISAGREE

Divide the group into three teams by counting off 1-2-3.

1. *Each team will identify a school-related issue in which some of the team members agree and some do not.*

   **What is your team's school-related issue?** _____

   _____

   **Read this quotation aloud and encourage each other to think independently.**

   When all think alike, no one thinks very much.
   **~ Walter Lippmann**

2. *Remember, it is okay to disagree. It is HOW you disagree that is important.*
   *Have fun discussing an issue with these guidelines:*
   - Risk voicing your opinions, knowing others will disagree.
   - Listen open-mindedly to opposing ideas without trying to change people's views.
   - Respect everyone's rights to speak without interruptions or put-downs.
   - Avoid raising your voice.
   - Stay clear of becoming angry.

3. *Afterward, evaluate your own actions using the scale #1 = minimal and #10 = maximal.*
   _____ My level of risk-taking.
   _____ My level of open-mindedness.
   _____ My level of respect toward people with different views.
   _____ My level of trust toward the team members as a whole.

4. *Using the same scale, estimate how the team functioned as a whole:*
   _____ Team's level of risk-taking.
   _____ Team's level of open-mindedness.
   _____ Team's level of respect toward people with different views.
   _____ Team's level of trust toward the team members as a whole.

5. *Now, confer with team members to find out about their scale rating activity:*
   - Ratings of the team's function as a whole.
   - Observations about the team experience.

*Remember: it is okay to agree to disagree!*

# Agree to Disagree – Facilitator Possibilities

### Strengths and Opportunities
Evaluate one's own actions and peers' interactions regarding risk-taking, open-mindedness, respect, and level of trust.

### Supplies
Agree to Disagree handout and pens.

### Inquisitive Minds
Ask, "What school-related issues do you disagree about the most?"

### Suggestions
Divide the participants into teams as suggested on the Agree to Disagree handout.
Distribute the Agree to Disagree handout to each participant.
Call their attention to Numbers 1 and 2 on the handout.
Teams complete Numbers 1 and 2 for ten or fifteen minutes.
Teams remain assembled but members privately complete Numbers 3 and 4.
Team members discuss Number 5.
All participants re-convene and spokespersons from each group share their team's experiences.

### Wrap-Up
Encourage discussion about: *The Pros and Cons of Agreeing to Disagree.*

### Independent and Team Projects

#### Independent
Individuals answer the questions from their team members regarding *an on-going or recent issue with family members, friends, etc.* Discuss differences of opinion among team members.

#### Team
The page as presented is a team activity.

#### Individuals or Teams
Individuals journal and teams discuss their positive and negative experiences with groups of people who think alike versus those whose members think differently. Remind them to be respectful.

# STRATEGIES FOR CONFLICT RESOLUTION

There is no BEST way to resolve conflicts.
There are many different valid conflict resolution strategies,
dependent on the appropriate reason, people involved, time, and place.

**Accommodate** — to give in when the issue is unimportant to one party.
*Ex: A person who likes most foods agrees to a friend's restaurant preference.*

**Avoid** — to dodge an issue when the annoyance or relationship is unimportant.
*Ex: A viewer changes seats at a movie when annoyed by a talkative stranger.*

**Collaborate** — to cooperate, understand both or all sides, and achieve a win-win solution.
*Ex: Teammates disagree about strategies and create a new game plan agreeable to all.*

**Compromise** – to partially satisfy each side and be acceptable to both.
*Ex: A teen wants a 1 a.m. curfew and parents/caregivers say 11 p.m.; they compromise on midnight.*

**Force** — to use power and authority.
*Ex: A parent pulls back a three-year-old who is running toward the street.*

**The BEST strategy to use depends on these factors:**

- The importance of the issue.
- The importance of the relationship.
- The balance of power.
- The amount of time available.

A volunteer will write each of the words below on a separate piece of paper.
Then, place them in a container.

**Accommodate    Avoid    Collaborate    Compromise    Force**

**Divide into five teams.**
*Each team picks out one piece of paper (no looking ahead!)
Then, each team will improvise a skit that shows a situation
in which their strategy is most effective.*

**Jot down your team's ideas here:**

*Now, each team will have fun performing their skit for the other four teams.*

# STRATEGIES FOR CONFLICT RESOLUTION – FACILITATOR POSSIBILITIES

**Strengths and Opportunities**
Identify conflict resolution strategies and circumstances in which each strategy is appropriate.

**Supplies**
Strategies for Conflict Resolution handout and pens.
Five slips of paper and a container.

**Inquisitive Minds**
Ask, "What is improvisational theater or improv?"
*Example: Using the phrase, "Yes, and" to affirm and build upon what another person has said, even if you don't agree with their statement.*

**Suggestions**
Distribute the Strategies for Conflict Resolution handouts.
Review information and directions.
Participants form teams.
Teams confer briefly to discuss their improvisation.
Advise teams to limit their performances to a few minutes.
After each skit, other teams guess the strategy portrayed and discuss its appropriateness for the situation.

**Wrap-Up**
Participants discuss which strategy to use in situations where there is NOT a balance of power.
*Ex: A teen disagrees with a school rule but goes along with it. Later, the teen may bring it up at a student council meeting with the hopes that they can all collaborate to modify or change the rule.*

**Independent and Team Projects**
**Independent**
Individuals compose scenarios to demonstrate which strategy would be most effective.

**Team**
The page as presented is a team activity.

**Individuals or Teams**
Individuals journal and teams discuss times they used an effective strategy to resolve a conflict.
Individuals or teams create humorous stories whose characters use inappropriate strategies.

**TEAM PLAYER** — Gifted and Talented Teens Workbook

# TIME TO ADAPT?

Imagine you are on a team and you need to respond.

*Example:*
*Team-like Scenario: any group of people – family members, friends, sport team, choir, etc.*
*You are in a backstage theater group and have great ideas for the best stage design.*

**Which way would you respond?**
- Stay in the dark = you keep quiet to avoid appearing arrogant and allow a flawed design.
- Shine your light = strongly express your expertise and quit if you don't get your way.
- Adapt = you share your ideas respectfully, listen to others, then accept the consensus.
- Adapt = you decide to leave or involve a trusted adult if their design could be harmful.

Compose a scenario in the top box; do not write in the bottom box.
Your scenario will be shared with others who will state their responses.

| Team-like Scenario |
|---|
|   |

**Stay in the dark =**

**Shine your light =**

**Adapt =**

**Other adaptive responses =**

# Time to Adapt? – Facilitator Possibilities

**Strengths and Opportunities**
Explore the symbolic meaning of *staying in the dark* and *shining one's light*.

**Supplies**
Time to Adapt handout and pens.

**Inquisitive Minds**
Ask, "What is the symbolic meaning of shining one's light?"
*Lead them to the definition above: to strongly express your expertise and quit if you don't get your way. Alternatively, to tower over others intellectually.*

**Suggestions**
Distribute the Time to Adapt handout.
After completion, participants use the page as a Flashcard or play Pass the Paper.
*Flashcard: The writer reads the scenario aloud and calls on volunteers who each state one response.*
*Pass the Paper: Participants pass their scenarios to three adjacent peers who each write one response.*

**Wrap-Up**
Participants discuss stories of times they used each of these strategies:
Stayed in the dark
Shone their light
Adapted

**Independent and Team Projects**

**Independent**
Individuals complete the entire page as a journaling exercise; volunteers share their responses.

**Team**
The page as presented is a team activity.

**Individuals or Teams**
Create an acrostic related to team-like adaptation.
*Example:*
**A** - Ask questions to help you understand others' views, not to intimidate them.
**D** - Determine when to: promote your views; back off; leave an unethical or unhealthy team.
**A** - Assert your opinion respectfully.
**P** - Perceive others' reactions to your ideas.
**T** - Tactfully let the team's consensus evolve, unless it could be harmful, unsafe, illegal, etc.

**TEAM PLAYER** — Gifted and Talented Teens Workbook

# Sportsmanship Messages

**Director's Lines:**
Messages are conveyed verbally, non-verbally, and through questions and answers.
You will send and receive messages about sportsmanship, important for team players.
If you receive a Pantomime script, use actions only, and your audience will guess the message.
If you receive a Verbal Role Play script, recruit another actor if necessary, improvise your speaking parts, and your audience will guess the message.
If you receive an Ask the Audience script, pose the question, and encourage a few viewers to share their opinions.
The only rules are: No violent or profane gestures or words. Have fun!

### Specific Scripts

✂------------------------------------------------------------------------------------

**Pantomime:** It's NOT okay for a teammate to make a mistake.

✂------------------------------------------------------------------------------------

**Pantomime:** It IS okay for as teammate to make a mistake.

✂------------------------------------------------------------------------------------

**Pantomime:** A conceited winner.

✂------------------------------------------------------------------------------------

**Verbal Role Play:** A humble winner.

✂------------------------------------------------------------------------------------

**Pantomime:** A poor loser.

✂------------------------------------------------------------------------------------

**Verbal Role Play:** A gracious loser.

✂------------------------------------------------------------------------------------

**Verbal Role Play:** The wrong way to react to a decision against your team.

✂------------------------------------------------------------------------------------

**Ask the audience:** Describe examples of good and bad sportsmanship that you have witnessed.

✂------------------------------------------------------------------------------------

**Ask the Audience:** Which contributes more to success – good luck or hard work and why?

✂------------------------------------------------------------------------------------

# SPORTSMANSHIP MESSAGES – Facilitator Possibilities

**Strengths and Opportunities**
Recognize the effects of positive and negative sportsmanship.

**Supplies**
Scissors.

**Inquisitive Minds**
Ask, "What is non-verbal communication?" (Facial expression, body language, etc.)
Ask, "Give some examples of non-verbal communication that shows real feelings while words may cover the truth." *(A person's eyes have tears in them as the person says, "I'm fine.")*

**Suggestions**
Before the session, photocopy one handout and cut on the dotted lines for the director's lines and scripts.
Ask for a volunteer to be the director.
Give the Director's Lines cutout to the volunteer, who will read the lines aloud.
Place the script cutouts face down.
A volunteer picks up a cutout and follows the instructions, recruiting a partner as needed for the scene.
The volunteer(s) pantomime or role play and the audience guesses their message.
Participants who pick up *Ask the Audience*, elicit a few responses.
Continue until all cutouts are used.

**Wrap-Up**
A volunteer writes the heading Teams Unrelated to Sports on the board and lists participants' ideas.
   *Ex: A work team.*
Another volunteer calls on peers to identify ways to be a team player for each item listed.
   *Ex: Help train a new coworker.*

**Independent and Team Projects**
   **Independent**
      Individuals receive the uncut handout and write descriptions of pantomimes and role plays.
      Individuals respond in writing to the Ask the Audience questions.
      Individuals journal about their experiences as a team player.

   **Team**
      The page as presented is a team activity.

   **Individuals or Teams**
      Research examples of good and bad sportsmanship at awards ceremonies, the Olympics, favorite sports teams, and other competitions. Volunteers share their findings.

# Everyone Makes Mistakes!

Making mistakes is a normal part of life! Taking responsibility, learning from our mistakes without dwelling on them, being aware that other people also make mistakes, and not harshly blaming oneself or anyone else is the ultimate goal!

Fables are short stories about animals or other creatures with human qualities. Fables demonstrate a life lesson and end with a slogan, motto, or words of wisdom (the moral of the story) about behavior. **Create a fable about a "star" who played perfectly, lost, and blamed the loss on someone else's mistake.** Your "star" can be in sports, entertainment, academic competition, orchestra, debate, or any other setting.

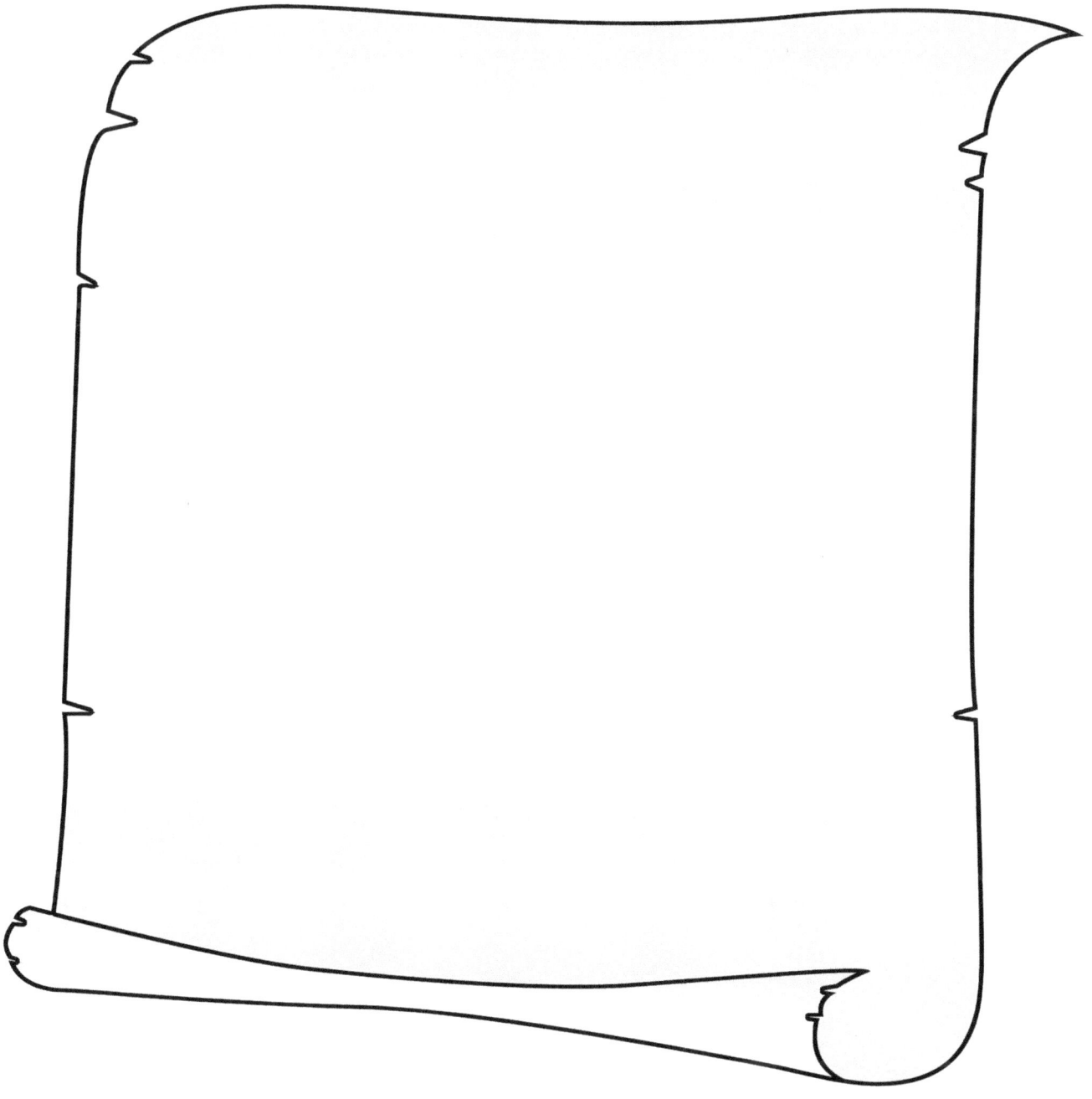

# Everyone Makes Mistakes! – Facilitator Possibilities

**Strengths and Opportunities**
    Identify the possible repercussions of blaming someone else for one's loss.
    Recognize that a mistake could be made by oneself.
    Acknowledge that mistakes are often learning experiences.

**Supplies**
    Everyone Makes Mistakes handouts and pens.

**Inquisitive Minds**
    Ask, "What is the meaning of *'People in glass houses shouldn't throw stones.'*?"
    *(Don't criticize others for faults you may have.)*
    Accept any interpretations; note that it is a about a slogan, motto, or words of wisdom about behavior (the moral of the story).

**Suggestions**
    Distribute the Everyone Makes Mistakes handout.
    Participants complete the page.
    Volunteers read their fables aloud.

**Wrap-Up**
    The group creates a fable to illustrate the following message in a positive way:
    *Ex: Mistakes are learning experiences.*

**Independent and Team Projects**
  **Independent**
    The page as presented is an independent project.

  **Team**
    Teams create and enact fables.
    Audience members discuss possible catchphrases for the moral of the story.

  **Individuals or Teams**
    Individuals journal and teams discuss times they made mistakes and ways others comforted or criticized them.
    Individuals journal and teams discuss their reactions to friends' and family members' mistakes.

# Not Everyone Gets the Gold

Imagine you worked your whole life toward winning an Olympic Gold Medal.
You get to the Olympics and you don't get the gold, or silver, or bronze.

*Apply this quotation to the above situation:*

> "There are victories of the soul and spirit.
> Sometimes, even if you lose, you win."
> ~ Elie Wiesel

**How would the quote in the box above apply to you if you were the person who didn't earn a medal?**

_____
_____

**Imagine that a member of your country's team won the gold medal.**

What would you want to say to this person? _____
_____

What do you think you would say to this person? _____
_____

What would you ask this person? _____
_____

How could you discover what your strengths were in this competition? _____
_____

How could you discover what your weaknesses were in this competition? _____
_____

Do you think you would want to give up and find a new passion? Explain. _____
_____

Do you think you would keep on trying for that medal? Explain. _____
_____

**Imagine that you won the gold medal!**

*On a blank piece of paper, journal your thoughts and feelings that contributed to your win.*

# NOT EVERYONE GETS THE GOLD – FACILITATOR POSSIBILITIES

**Strengths and Opportunities**
    Identify the possible positive outcomes as a result of a loss.
    Acknowledge one's own thoughts, feelings, and actions when winning.

**Supplies**
    Not Everyone Gets the Gold handout and pens.

**Inquisitive Minds**
    Ask, "What are your favorite Olympic sports?"
    Ask, "How would you describe the emotional roller coaster an Olympic athlete might experience?"

**Suggestions**
    Distribute the Not Everyone Gets the Gold handout.
    After completion, volunteers share their responses.

**Wrap-Up**
    Participants collaborate about non-sports situations when they could not get their way as a team member.
    *(Lose an election for class president, miss out on a promotion at work, etc.)*
    Volunteers take turns responding to the handout questions in a situation meaningful to them.

**Independent and Team Projects**
    **Independent**
        The page as presented is an individual project.

    **Team**
        Three teams each respond to one of the sections of the handout, then share with the group.

    **Individuals or Teams**
        Research Olympians who overcame losses, injuries, and other setbacks and report findings to the group.
        Research the purpose of, and inspiring stories about, the Paralympics.

# FOLLOWERSHIP POWER

Followership, like leadership, is a role and not a destination.
~ Michael McKinney

**Consider these Followership Power concepts:**

- Followers have power when they give energy and activism to a leader they support,
    **and** ... when they respectfully express their own beliefs.
- Followers have power when they pay attention to the leader's words, and actions,
    **and** ...when they question the leader's motives if necessary.
- Followers have power when they understand opposing views,
    **and** ... when they change their own opinions if warranted, based on new information.
- Followers have power when they give credit to deserving leaders,
    **and** ... when they recognize their own contributions.
- Followers have power when they know their position in the chain of command,
    **and** ... when they use the chain of command to convey their ideas.

Complete the columns to highlight your follower roles.

| Person in Authority<br>(Ex: Mom or Dad, Teacher, Coach) | Rules I Must Follow At This Time | Ways I Can Respectfully Try To Initiate Change | Ways I Could Lead |
|---|---|---|---|
| Home | | | |
| School and/or Extra-Curricular Activities | | | |
| Work and/or Volunteer Job | | | |
| Elsewhere | | | |

On a blank paper, describe your experiences
with each of the bulleted items in the top section of this page.

# Followership Power - Facilitator Possibilities

**Strengths and Opportunities**
>Acknowledge personal examples of follower power.
>Identify follower situations, rules, and respectful ways to initiate change.
>Identify ways to lead.

**Supplies**
>Followership Power handout and pens.

**Inquisitive Minds**
>Ask, "Will a few volunteers please demonstrate a *Simon Says* game?"
>Instructions:
>1. Choose someone to be Simon.
>2. Have Simon give a command to the other players.
>3. If the command starts with "Simon Says," the players have to do it.
>4. If the command does NOT start with "Simon Says", and a player does it, the player is OUT!
>5. The last person standing wins.
>
>Ask, "When does it make sense to follow a leader?"
>Ask, "When does it NOT make sense to follow a leader?"
>Elicit that sometimes people must submit to authority unless they or others could be harmed.
>*Ex: Parent/caregiver rules; school, workplace, sports team, and club policies.*

**Suggestions**
>Distribute the Followership Power handouts.
>After completion, volunteers share their responses.

**Wrap-Up**
>Participants brainstorm ways to respectfully initiate positive change:
>*Ex: Research the issue, appeal to heads and hearts along the chain of command, recruit problem-solving peers, not just complainers, enlist support from experts on the issue.*

**Independent and Team Projects**

**Independent**
>The page as presented is an individual project.

**Team**
>One team researches followers who have allowed themselves to be led into disastrous situations.
>One team researches student activists who worked toward a positive change in school safety.

**Individuals or Teams**
>Individuals journal and teams discuss stories about times they followed a leader and…
>>experienced a negative outcome.
>>experienced a positive outcome.

# Challenge the Leader

## LEADERS

*Think about the following words of wisdom:*

Real joy comes not from ease or riches or from the praise of men,
but from doing something worthwhile.
### ~ Sir Wilfred Grenfell

You have the opportunity of a lifetime – to fulfill your wildest dream – to make a difference!

**Meet with your team and ...**
- Consider opposing opinions.
- Create a plan.
- Empower through delegation.
- Encourage members' participation.
- Express trust in members' abilities.
- Help resolve conflicts.
- Inspire innovative ideas.
- Keep hope alive.
- Share your vision.

## TEAM MEMBERS WHO CHALLENGE A LEADER

*Think about these words of wisdom:*

Real joy comes not from ease or riches or from the praise of men,
but from doing something worthwhile.
### ~ Sir Wilfred Grenfell

**Take turns portraying behaviors that challenge the leader...**
- Ask for the leader's vision.
- Complain about assigned tasks.
- Describe the best and worst possible outcomes.
- Disagree about a plan without listening to the entire proposal.
- Explain why you have lost hope, or have renewed hope, for a successful outcome.
- Express doubt to others about the leader's abilities.
- Insist on the same old solutions and offer some new ones.
- Oppose some of the leader's opinions and support others.
- Praise the leader in front of others.
- Suggest realistic ideas.

# Challenge the Leader – Facilitator Possibilities

**Strengths and Opportunities**
    Identify characteristics of leadership skills.
    Identify different ways to challenge the leader, both negative and positive.

**Supplies**
    Challenge the Leader handout and pens.
    Scissors for facilitator to cut the broken line on the handouts.

**Inquisitive Minds**
    Ask, "What are some qualities of effective leaders?"
        *(Honest, imaginative, courageous, open-minded, etc.).*
    Ask, "What are some bad behaviors of team members who challenge a leader?"
        *(Narrow-minded, argumentative, disrespectful, apathetic, etc.)*

**Suggestions**
    Before the session, photocopy Challenge the Leader handout and cut them on the broken line.
    Explain that participants will take part in a simulation, or imitation of a leadership-team process.
    Some participants will volunteer to play leaders; others will portray team members.
    Remind them to be respectful.
    Distribute the LEADERS handout to volunteer leaders.
    Distribute TEAM MEMBERS WHO CHALLENGE A LEADER handouts to the other participants.
    Neither team may see the others' handouts.
    Decide on one of the following options:
        Each leader takes a turn working with the whole group of challenging team members.
        If there are large numbers of teens and space, each leader works with a set of team members.
        Ask the leaders to decide on their role (class president, etc.) and vision (improve school safety, etc.).
        Allow about ten to fifteen minutes per leader and team to enact the simulation.
        Encourage participants to share their thoughts and feelings about their roles.

**Wrap-Up**
    Refer participants to the quotation on their handouts.
    Ask volunteers to describe what "doing something worthwhile" means to them.

**Independent and Team Projects**
    **Independent**
        Participants use the prompts to write scripts for a leader and challenging team members.
        Volunteers read their scripts aloud or make copies for peers to speak the parts.

    **Team**
        The page as presented is a team project.

    **Individuals or Teams**
        Individuals journal, or teams discuss, the most challenging and the most enjoyable aspects of their real-life experiences as team leaders.

# COMMUNICATION: HEART OR HEAD FIRST?

People are in relationships with friends, family, neighbors,
co-workers, and/or partners.

*Consider this scenario:*

*Your friend is devastated over a breakup and shares it with you.
Your head's logic may say: "You'll find someone better." or "I didn't like him anyway."
Your heart's empathy might say: "This must really hurt."*

*Now respond to this scenario as you believe you would in real life:*

Your logical head would say: _____
_____

Your empathetic heart would say: _____
_____

Which would be your initial response to your friend and why? _____
_____
_____

*As a logical person, your head wants to solve the person's problems,
but that person may not want a solution, at least not yet!
That person may want your empathy more than your logic or advice.*

*On a separate piece of paper describe a scenario of your own in which you are experiencing stress or a disappointment.*
*On the back, write how you would like someone to respond to you, when you share it. Do not use actual names.*

# Communication: Heart or Head First? – Facilitator Possibilities

**Strengths and Opportunities**
    Identify logical and empathetic responses.
    Exemplify intellectual and emotional self-talk.

**Supplies**
    Communication: Heart or Head First? handout and pens.
    Scissors to cut the broken line on the handouts, or teens may tear paper at the line.

**Inquisitive Minds**
    Ask, "When someone you know has a problem, what do you usually do first?"
    Participants may try to solve the problem, help the person, etc.
    Ask, "What do you think the person with the problem wants from you?"
    Participants may say that the person wants solutions, support, etc.

**Suggestions**
    Distribute the Communication: Heart or Head First? handout and discuss the scenario.
    Participants respond to the sentences below.
    Volunteers share their responses.
    Participants read the scenario, and complete their response.
    The responses are collected, shuffled, and stacked at the front of the room.
    Participants take turns doing the following:
        Pick up a scenario and read it aloud.
        Ask for volunteers to state possible heart and head responses.
    After listening to a few responses from the group, turn the scenario over and read the written response aloud.
    Encourage peers to discuss the pros and cons of logic versus empathy after each scenario.

**Wrap-Up**
    Volunteers share a challenge they now face and their logical and empathetic self-talk.

**Independent and Team Projects**
  **Independent**
      The page as presented is an independent activity up to the scenario at the bottom of the page.
      Individuals list their own heart and head responses on a blank sheet of paper.

  **Team**
      The scenarios are distributed to volunteer panels.
      Panel members read aloud the scenarios, discuss possible head and heart responses in front of the whole group, and then read aloud the original solution.

  **Individuals or Teams**
      Individuals journal, or teams discuss situations in which they experienced challenges and the responses that people made that were unhelpful and helpful.

# TOO Easily Offended?

> **CAUTION!**
> Awareness of your own feelings and sensitivity to others' feelings is certainly a positive quality. However, mean-spirited put-downs and name-calling, as well as threats, physical violence, inappropriate sexual contact, harm, and other forms of ABUSE to be REPORTED TO A TRUSTED ADULT.

### Are You TOO Easily Offended?

If you become angry over almost anything; if you take things too personally; if you experience hurt feelings way too often; or if others say they *walk on eggshells* around you or that you are *high maintenance,* you may be TOO easily offended. It is unhealthy for you and for your relationships when you constantly take things personally and have hurt feelings over things that other people say or do.

**Describe a situation in which you may have been too easily offended.**

_____
_____
_____

1. If you were criticized, was any part of it true? _____ Explain. _____
   _____

2. If the person had worded it differently, would that have made it okay? _____ Explain. _____
   _____

3. Were the words or actions possibly related to the person's own problems? (jealous? bad day? didn't understand what you said?) _____ Explain. _____
   _____

4. Below, draw a comic strip of someone who says something that offends you and you are superhero! When you put on your cloak, you are protected from being easily offended.

|   |   |   |   |
|---|---|---|---|
|   |   |   |   |

*When someone says something rude or thoughtless, visualize yourself wearing your imaginary superhero cloak and let those words just roll off of your cloak!*

# TOO EASILY OFFENDED? – FACILITATOR POSSIBILITIES

**Strengths and Opportunities**
    Acknowledge that being aware of feelings is a positive trait.
    Acknowledge that being offended by abuse is imperative.
    Recognize signs of being easily and /or inappropriately offended.

**Supplies**
    Too Easily Offended? handout and pens.

**Inquisitive Minds**
    Ask, "In what ways does social media contribute to hurt feelings?"
        *(Bullying; gossiping that spreads quickly; comments are easily misinterpreted without the ability to see facial expression, hear the tone of a voice, etc.)*
    Ask, "Can other people hurt your feelings?" (Not without your permission.)
    Ask, "What does it mean to let an insult be 'Like water off a duck's back.' ?"
        *(To ignore it, to NOT let it penetrate your identity.)*

**Suggestions**
    Distribute Too Easily Offended? handout.
    Read aloud the **"CAUTION"** box on the top of the page, and briefly discuss the information.
    Participants complete the page.
    Volunteers share their responses
    .

**Wrap-Up**
    Copy the following quotation onto the board:
        "We should be too big to take offense and too noble to give it." ~ Abraham Lincoln
    Ask volunteers to share stories about times they behaved in these ways:
        Took offence over small stuff.
        Did or said something that someone perceived as offensive.
        Were too noble to say or do something that could be perceived as offensive.

**Independent and Team Projects**
    **Independent**
        Individuals journal about times they learned from constructive criticism.

    **Team**
        Teams discuss situations in which they gave, or wanted to give, constructive criticism to someone they cared about.

    **Individuals or Teams**
        Research famous people who pursued their passions and stuck to their beliefs despite criticism.

# CHAPTER 5

# Self-Expression

> Self-Expression is a way of conveying your thoughts, feelings, and opinions; exhibiting your personality; and bringing out your spirit and true character. One way you express your individuality is through the way you dress, your hairstyle, etc. You express yourself through your unique gifts and talents: speech, the written word, art, music, drama, theater, photography, or any other method you choose to carry your message.
>
> Self-expression motivates you to develop your insight, your view of the world, and your personal power, as well as to communicate your personal truths for others to consider.

There is a vitality, a life force, an energy, a quickening
that is translated thoroughly through you into action,
and because there is only one of you in all of time,
this expression is unique. And if you block it,
it will never exist through any other medium
and it will be lost.
~ **Martha Graham**

---

In this chapter teens share ideas about topics important to them through their choices of visual art, the written or spoken word, theater, dance, music, fantasy, and other techniques. Teens change self-limiting thoughts into personal power, identify insights, evoke emotions, and take healthy risks through creative expression.

# Your World

**Examples of Self-Expression**
*Compose lyrics, poetry, prose, fiction, a journal entry, blog, an essay,
dance routine, pantomime, or role-play.
Draw a caricature, cartoon, collage, poster, or sculpture.
Sing, play an instrument, or compose a rap.
Write or perform in a dramatic or humorous skit.
Use any other technique that expresses your thoughts and feelings!*

*In the box below, express ways the following quotation is
true and/or untrue in your world.*

Here is the world.
Beautiful and terrible things will happen.
Don't be afraid.
~ **Frederick Buechner**

*Being scared is an opportunity to be brave.*

**Gifted and Talented Teens Workbook — SELF-EXPRESSION**

# Your World — Facilitator Possibilities

**Strengths and Opportunities**
    Express an idea creatively in one's own personal way.
    Identify ways terrible experiences can illustrate beauty.

**Supplies**
    Your World handout and pens.

**Inquisitive Minds**
    Ask participants to give examples of life experiences that are opposites.
        *(Ex: Win or lose a game; feel accepted or rejected by others.)*

**Suggestions**
    Distribute the Your World handout.
    A volunteer reads the text in the box aloud, and then the quotation.
    Emphasize: Participants may create their own self-expression technique or use one of the examples.

**Wrap-Up**
    Write on the board: **Here is the world.**
    Participants suggest ideas about the next three lines that could follow.
        Example:
        *You will experience harmony and discord.*
        *You will hear truth and lies.*
        *Don't be surprised.*

**Independent and Team Projects**

    **Independent**
        The page as presented is an independent project.

    **Team**
        Teams discuss, debate, or create a storyboard, mural, song, play, etc.

    **Individuals or Teams**
        Individuals list ways terrible experiences can illustrate beauty.
        Teams discuss ways terrible experiences can illustrate beauty.
        Possibilities:
            *Flowers that spring up after forest fires.*
            *Heroes who emerge despite disasters.*

# Individualized Initialisms

In the box below, use the following initialisms to inspire a blog that expresses your opinions on a certain topic. Use your creativity to write new initialisms or incorporate those below. If you need more space write on the other side of this sheet.

**ASAP** — *As Soon As Possible* _____

**BTW** — *By The Way* _____

**FYI** — *For Your Information* _____

**IMO** — *In My Opinion* _____

**IRL** — *In Real Life* _____

**LOL** — *Laughing Out Loud* _____

**NTS** — *Note To Self* _____

**Q&A** — *Question and Answer* _____

**R&R** — *Rest and Relaxation* _____

**RPG** — *Role Playing Game* _____

**SMH** — *Shaking My Head* _____

**SOP** — *Standard Operating Procedure* _____

**TBA** — *To Be Announced* _____

**TLC** — *Tender Loving Care* _____

**VIP** — *Very Important Person* _____

**VSF** — *Very Sad Face* _____

**WOM** — *Word Of Mouth* _____

MY TOPIC _____

MY BLOG ABOUT THIS TOPIC _____

_____

_____

_____

_____

_____

_____

_____

_____

# Individualized Initialisms — Facilitator Possibilities

**Strengths and Opportunities**
    Formulate opinions by personalizing and/or creating initialisms or acronyms.

**Supplies**
    Individualized Initialisms handout and pens.

**Inquisitive Minds**
    What is the difference between an initialism, an acronym, and an abbreviation?
        An initialism abbreviates a series of words to be spoken as letters.
            *Ex: FBI – Federal Bureau of Investigation*
        An acronym uses the first letters but is pronounced as a word.
            *Ex: RADAR – Radio Detection and Ranging*
        An abbreviation is a shortened form of a word.
            *Ex: AVE or AV – Avenue*

**Suggestions**
    Distribute the Individualized Initialisms handout.
    After completion, volunteers share their blogs.

**Wrap-Up**
    Ask participants to underline their most surprising response to an initialism.
    Volunteers share their responses and explain why they were surprised.

**Independent and Team Projects**
    **Independent**
        The page as presented is an independent project.

    **Team**
        Teams complete the handout, and then share their responses with other teams.

    **Individuals or Teams**
        Individuals list and teams suggest acronyms. They may make up their own.
            *Ex: FEAR – False Evidence Appearing Real.*
        Individuals journal and teams discuss insights gained from acronyms.
            *Ex: FEAR – Someone fears people in a huddle are talking about him/her, but the group is actually planning a surprise party for the person.*

# Teen Culture

## You meet a creature from another galaxy who asks about teen culture on Planet Earth.

*Describe your typical teen culture by using
a collage of sketches, icons, lyrics, prose, or any creative expression.
Incorporate any items from the list below and/or your own categories.
These are only listed as starting points. Use a separate sheet of paper.*

| | | | |
|---|---|---|---|
| Appearance | Dating | School | Technology |
| Attitudes | Family | Social media | Values |
| Behavior | Friends | Sports | Vocabulary |
| Beliefs | Music | Styles | |

## The creature is from a planet named Utopia.

On another sheet of paper, depict and describe the creature's
explanation of the Utopian (ideal) teen culture.

# Teen Culture — Facilitator Possibilities

**Strengths and Opportunities**
>Discover a personal view of both the typical and ideal teen cultures.
>Identify ways to personally and collaboratively facilitate a more positive teen culture.
>Be sure everyone understands what a utopian culture means.

**Supplies**
>Teen Culture handout and pens.
>Optional: Art supplies and drawing paper.

**Inquisitive Minds**
>Ask, "Are science fiction movies a waste of time or a creative experience?" Explain.

**Suggestions**
>Distribute the Teen Culture handout, optional art supplies, and paper.
>After completion, volunteers share their responses on the handout.
>Write this heading on the board, "Utopian Teen Culture"
>A volunteer elicits and lists peers' responses from the separate pieces of paper.
>The group discusses actions they can take to make the typical teen culture more ideal than it is presently.
>*Possibilities:*
>>Invite a new student to their lunch table.
>>Raise funds to pay for music lessons and/or instruments for teens who cannot afford the cost.

**Wrap-Up**
>Encourage a discussion of ways participants are different, and the ways they are the same as the typical teen culture and why.

**Independent and Team Projects**
>**Independent**
>>The page as presented is an independent project.
>
>**Team**
>>Teams create depictions and descriptions of typical and ideal teen cultures.
>>Volunteers from each team present their responses to the group.
>
>**Individuals or Teams**
>>Research ways teens might try to improve their culture in the near future.
>>>*Ex: Peaceful assembly regarding any teen issue.*

# Speak Your Truth

Don't cry because it's over — smile because it happened.
### ~ Theodore Seuss Geisel (Dr. Seuss)

Some people disagree with, "Don't cry because it's over."
They believe grief and tears are a healthy initial response to loss.
Their truth might be, *"Cry because it's over, **and then** smile because it happened."*

*Recall or research a quotation that does not seem quite true to you.*

_____

_____

*Explain your reasons.*

_____

_____

*Speak your truth by changing the quotation.*

_____

_____

*Imagine…*
  *You are a famous person whose words will be respected and repeated for centuries.*
  *Consider an issue that is important to you.*
  *Compose your own statement that speaks your truth.*

# Speak Your Truth — Facilitator Possibilities

**Strengths and Opportunities**
    Formulate words of wisdom about an issue of personal importance.
    Find ways to promote personal truth.

**Supplies**
    Speak Your Truth handout and pens.

**Inquisitive Minds**
    Ask participants to give examples of words of wisdom that they think are controversial.
    *(Ex: Everything happens for the best is often questioned during tragedies.)*

**Suggestions**
    Distribute the Speak Your Truth handout.
    Participants recall or research a famous quotation.
    After completion, volunteers share their responses.

**Wrap-Up**
    Encourage a discussion of multimedia methods to promote participants' truths.
    *Possibilities:*
        Add the quote to email signatures, create social media posts, texts, etc.
        Create a poster incorporating the text with relevant art work.
        Perform a simulated TV infomercial.
        Compose music and lyrics, a play, or a short story that incorporates the quotation.

**Independent and Team Projects**
    **Independent**
        The page as presented is an independent project.

    **Team**
        Pairs of participants or teams complete the page collaboratively.
        Volunteers from each pair or team present their responses to the group.

    **Individuals or Teams**
        Make up or research controversial quotations and share them with the group.
        Peers debate about the reasons they agree or disagree with the quotations.

# Entelechy = YOU!

A caterpillar becomes a butterfly; a kernel explodes into popcorn. Why?

**Entelechy! (en-'te-lə-kē) = that which turns potential into reality.**

Genetic codes and environmental conditions control caterpillars and corn.
These codes and conditions can help you too, but...
**YOU = that which turns your potential into reality.**

### Examples of Self-Expression

- Compose music lyrics, a dance routine, poetry, prose, fiction, a journal entry, blog, or an essay.
- Create a new game.
- Dance, pantomime, or role play.
- Draw a caricature, cartoon, collage, poster, or sculpture.
- Sing, play an instrument, or rap.
- Write or perform in a dramatic or humorous skit.
- Any other technique that describes your thoughts and feelings!

*Choose any methods of self-expression and describe below.*

**My thoughts, feelings, and actions, which will turn my potential into reality:**

# Entelechy = YOU! — Facilitator Possibilities

**Strengths and Opportunities**
    Acknowledge how one can turn personal potential into reality through thoughts, feelings, and actions.
      Identify external and internal factors that contribute to reaching one's potential.

**Supplies**
    Entelechy = YOU! handout and pens.
    Optional: Art supplies, musical instruments, space to practice and perform a song, skit, etc.

**Inquisitive Minds**
    Ask, "How does a caterpillar become a butterfly?"
      *(Inside the chrysalis it digests itself using enzymes triggered by hormones.*
      *Then sleeping cells grow into body parts of the future butterfly).*
    Ask, "How do you become what you can be?" (Accept any answers.)
    Allow a brief discussion about the role of heredity and environment.

**Suggestions**
    Distribute the handout and any optional supplies.
    After completion, volunteers share their responses.

**Wrap-Up**
    Create two columns on the board with the headings: External Factors and Internal Factors.
    A volunteer leads a discussion session by eliciting and listing peer ideas re: external and internal factors that contribute to reaching one's highest potential.
    *Possibilities:*
      External: caregiver encouragement, quality education, resources (Internet, cultural, etc.)
      Internal: motivation, mental and physical health, belief in self, curiosity, a passion, etc.).

**Independent and Team Projects**
    **Independent**
      The page as presented is an independent project.

    **Team**
      Participants form teams depending on their interests: art, music, prose, poetry, theater, etc.
      Each team depicts, describes, sings, performs, etc., showing ways to turn potential into reality.

    **Individuals or Teams**
      Research biographies of people who excelled due to internal factors despite their external obstacles.

SELF-EXPRESSION — Gifted and Talented Teens Workbook

# Limiting or Limitless?

**As the story goes ...**
A baby elephant was chained to a big tree and could not break free. He stopped trying.
As an adult, he never tried to escape, even when tied to a tiny tree by a thin rope.
The elephant believed that he could not move beyond false boundaries.

*Depict and/or describe in each box:*

**My Self-Limiting Belief**

**How I Will Break Free**

**What I Will Be Doing When False Boundaries Are Gone**

# Limiting or Limitless? — Facilitator Possibilities

**Strengths and Opportunities**
    Examine a personal self-limiting belief.
    Identify ways to break free.
    Anticipate one's personal actions when false boundaries are gone.

**Supplies**
    Limiting or Limitless? handout and pens.

**Inquisitive Minds**
    Ask volunteers to share training techniques they have seen used with animals.
    Tell participants that they will read a story about a well-trained elephant.

**Suggestions**
    Distribute the Limiting or Limitless? handout.
    After completion, volunteers share their responses.

**Wrap-Up**
    Ask, "What could prevent teens from reaching their potential if they accept it?"
        *(Destructive criticism, negative self-talk, past setbacks, substance abuse, etc.)*
    Make four columns on the board with the following headings:
        *Intellectual Potential, Creative Potential, Social Potential, Mental Health Potential*
    A volunteer elicits and lists peers' ideas about ways to reach each potential

**Independent and Team Projects**
    **Independent**
        The page as presented is an independent project.

    **Team**
        Teens form four teams (Intellectual, Creative, Social, and Mental Health).
        Each team lists ways to develop their assigned potential.
        The group re-convenes and spokespersons from each team share their ideas.

    **Individuals or Teams**
        Research Self-Actualization and Maslow's Hierarchy of Needs.
            Individuals draw or journal about their progress up the hierarchy.
            Teams discuss or debate about the pros and cons of Maslow's theory.

# Q&A: Site for Insight

*Pretend you have developed a Question and Answer website.*

*Name your website: _____*

*Launch your site by asking the first question about an issue important to you.*
*Ex: Is college a must for every high school graduate? Explain.*

*Write your question in the question box.*

| Question |
|---|
|  |

- *After everyone writes one question, the papers are passed around the room.*
- *Everyone will answer two different questions.*
- *When you receive a paper, if you have insight into the issue, write one answer.*
- *If you prefer not to answer, pass the paper to the next person.*
- *The papers are claimed by their originators when each question has two answers.*

**Answer #1**

_____
_____
_____
_____
_____

**Answer #2**

_____
_____
_____
_____
_____

*Gifted and Talented Teens Workbook* — **SELF-EXPRESSION**

# Q&A: Site for Insight — Facilitator Possibilities

**Strengths and Opportunities**
    Identify an issue of personal importance.
    Gain insight by problem solving.

**Supplies**
    Q & A: Site for Insight handout and pens.

**Inquisitive Minds**
    Ask participants for a show of hands:
        "Have you ever visited a Question and Answer website?"
        "Have you ever asked or answered a question?"
    Encourage a few volunteers to share questions they asked and/or answered.

**Suggestions**
    Distribute the Q & A for Insight handout.
    Review the instructions above the Question and Answer box.

**Wrap-Up**
    The originators of the questions:
        Volunteer to read aloud the questions and answers.
        Silently evaluate whether to further consider the answers.
    Participants may verbalize additional answers and comments.

**Independent and Team Projects**
  **Independent**
      Individuals ask, and then provide two different answers to their own questions.
      Volunteers share their responses.

  **Team**
      The page as presented is a team activity.

  **Individuals or Teams**
      Individuals write and teams discuss the pros and cons of Q &A websites.
      Volunteers share their ideas.
      Possibilities
          *Pro – you gain different perspectives about your issue.*
          *Con – the people answering are not necessarily experts.*

# EVOKE

*To evoke is to bring out, to recall to the conscious mind, or to produce a reaction:*

- Feeling
- Memory
- Protest
- Vision
- Anything hidden within

*You can evoke reactions through any work of art:*

- Dance
- Drawing
- Monologue
- Musical score
- Photograph
- Poem
- Pretend video
- Sculpture
- Short story
- Lyrics
- Editorial
- Any other method

*Interestingly ...*
*You may evoke different reactions in different people who experience your work, and often different reactions than you expect!*

*Create any work of art to EVOKE and share with others.*

## EVOKE — Facilitator Possibilities

**Strengths and Opportunities**
    Evoke a reaction through art, dance, music, theater, literature, etc.
    Benefit from giving and receiving feedback.

**Supplies**
    Evoke handout and pens.
    Paper and art supplies.
    Smart phones to photograph anything in the room except people.
    Optional: Tell participants the day before this session to bring their musical instruments.

**Inquisitive Minds**
    Ask for volunteers to describe songs, movies, photos, poems, etc. that they react to emotionally.
    Ask participants to discuss the types of reactions that can result from any work of art:
        *Examples:*
        *Tears during a sad movie.*
        *Action when injustice is exposed.*
        *Joy related to a song.*

**Suggestions**
    Distribute the Evoke handout.
    Ask volunteers to read the text aloud.
    Explain:
        Photos of people may not be used.
        Music may be used if the participant writes the score, lyrics, or performs.
    Allow time for participants to create their works of art.
    Volunteers share their works.
    Peers may share their reactions (thoughts, feelings, calls to action).
    Peers may not criticize the mechanics or artistic aspects of the work.

**Wrap-Up**
    The creators of each work of art describe reactions:
        Their reactions to their own work.
        The reactions they expected to evoke from self and others.

**Independent and Team Projects**
  **Independent**
        The page as presented is an individual project.

  **Team**
        Teams:
        Art, Music, Dance, Theater, Literature, etc. research famous works that evoke reactions.

  **Individuals or Teams**
        Individuals journal and teams discuss works of art that have affected them.
        *Ex.: songs heard with a loved one; a movie that prompted further research; etc.*

# Paraprosdokians

> Pæ-rê-prahz-dok-i-êns
> Figures of speech in which the end of the sentence is surprising or causes the reader to reinterpret the first part.

*Example of a well-known saying:*
    If you can't beat them, join them.

*Example of a paraprosdokian using the above saying:*
    If you can't beat them ... learn how they won.

*Below are some well-known phrases. Under each phrase, create a paraprosdokian:*

*A person is known by the company he keeps.*
    A person is known by _____

*Great minds think alike.*
    Great minds _____

*He who hesitates is lost.*
    He who hesitates is _____

*Look before you leap.*
    Look before you _____

*All you need is love.*
    All you need is _____

Research or recall personally meaningful sayings to start, then create three of your own **paraprosdokians**; messages you want to put out to the universe.

1. _____
2. _____
3. _____

# Paraprosdokians — Facilitator Possibilities

**Strengths and Opportunities**
Identify ways to think out-of-the-box.

**Supplies**
Paraprosdokian handouts and pens.

**Inquisitive Minds**
Ask participants for a few examples of sayings they have heard or used.
*(No pain, no gain; actions speak louder than words, etc.)*

**Suggestions**
Distribute the Paraprosdokians handout.
After completion, volunteers share their paraprosdokians.

**Wrap-Up**
The group creates original first parts of sayings as a volunteer writes them on the board.
The group invents endings as a volunteer writes them on the board.
Examples:
  *The best part of being a teen is …*_____.
    *creating your own identity.*
  *The worst part of being a teen is …*_____.
    *deciding who you want to be.*

**Independent and Team Projects**

**Independent**
The page as presented is an individual project.

**Team**
All participants:
  Finish the first five lines.
  Start the bottom three lines.
  Pass their papers to the person next to them who completes those three lines.
  All participants receive their papers back and read aloud the lines completed by peers.

**Individuals or Teams**
Research sayings on topics of personal importance.
  Copy one they agree with and copy one with which they disagree and explain why.
  Volunteers read aloud the sayings.
  Peers state whether they agree or disagree with each saying and why.

SELF-EXPRESSION — Gifted and Talented Teens Workbook

# Creativity

Creativity takes courage. ~ **Henri Matisse**

*In what ways do you think creativity requires courage? Explain on the lines below.*

_____

_____

_____

Use Your Creativity *(originality, inspiration, vision, etc.)* in Two Ways

1. Make a statement that requires courage for you to convey.
   *Ex: You plan to pursue your dream career that people say is unrealistic.*

2. Choose a creative expression technique that requires courage for you to attempt.
   *Ex: If you usually write, combine a sketch and a pantomime to make your point.*

*You may choose whether or not you wish to share your work.*

**Suggestions:**
Explore ideas, hopes, personal truths, etc. that you may not have acknowledged.
If necessary, use your most comfortable expression technique first, to clarify your idea.
Then, move out of your comfort zone to try a different technique.

## IMPORTANT

> *You are encouraged to promote an idea or criticize an ideology but do not speak negatively about a person, group, or culture.*

Use
　　another
　　　　piece
　　　　　　of
　　　　　　　paper
　　　　　　　　and/or
　　　　　　　　　other
　　　　　　　　　　materials
　　　　　　　　　　　in order
　　　　　　　　　　　　to become
　　　　　　　　　　　　　courageously
　　　　　　　　　　　　　　creative!

# Creativity — Facilitator Possibilities

**Strengths and Opportunities**
    Nurture courage through creativity.

**Supplies**
    Creativity handout and pens.
        Paper, art supplies, and optional items (musical instruments, etc.)
        Space to practice a skit, dance, or other performance.

**Inquisitive Minds**
    Ask participants to discuss ways to be creative.
        *Examples:*
            *Visual arts, writing, music, theater, marketing, satire, sports strategies,*
            *and/or problem solving.*

**Suggestions**
    Distribute the Creativity handout and supplies.
    After completion, volunteers share their projects or performances.

**Wrap-Up**
    Ask participants, "Are you familiar with artist, Pierre-Auguste Renoir, who suffered severe pain in his hands but continued to paint?" Henri Matisse asked him why.
    Ask participants, "Why do YOU think he would paint despite pain?" (Accept any responses).
    Copy Renoir's answer below onto the board:
        ***The pain passes but the beauty remains.*** *~ Pierre-Auguste Renoir*
    Encourage participants to explore ways this can be true in other circumstances.
        Possibilities:
            Art, music, poetry, etc. that participants created during difficulties.
            Important insights gained because of problems.
            Forgiveness and trust rebuilt after relationship issues.
            Rebounds in sports teams after several losses.

**Independent and Team Projects**
**Independent**
        The page as presented is an individual project.

**Team**
        Teams explore people who made prized contributions despite personal problems: artists, writers, musicians, athletes, actors, comedians, scientists, humanitarians, etc.

**Individuals or Teams**
        Individuals journal and teams discuss positive outcomes that outlived personal problems.

Whole Person Associates is the leading publisher of training resources for professionals who empower people to create and maintain healthy lifestyles. Our creative resources will help you work effectively with your clients in the areas of stress management, wellness promotion, mental health, and life skills.

Please visit us at our web site: **WholePerson.com**.
You can check out our entire line of products, place an order, request our print catalog, and sign up for our monthly special notifications.

**Whole Person Associates**
800-247-6789
Books@WholePerson.com

www.ingramcontent.com/pod-product-compliance
Lightning Source LLC
Chambersburg PA
CBHW082125230426
43671CB00015B/2808